In
DEFENSE
of the
CORPORATION

In
DEFENSE
of the
CORPORATION

ROBERT HESSEN

HOOVER INSTITUTION PRESS
Stanford University, Stanford, California

Hoover Institution Publication 207

© 1979 by the Board of Trustees of the
   Leland Stanford Junior University
All rights reserved
International Standard Book Number: 0-8179-7072-x
Library of Congress Catalog Card Number: 78-24743
Printed in the United States of America
Sixth Printing, 1986.

Dedicated to Bea,
with love

Contents

Acknowledgments   ix

Prologue   xi

1. The Concession Theory of Corporations   1

2. Are Corporations Creatures of the State?   13

3. What is a Corporate Charter?   23

4. The Partnership-Corporation Continuum   35

5. The Ideal of Corporate Democracy   47

6. Why State Incorporation Laws Are Permissive   61

7. Are Shareholders Being Victimized?   77

8. Breaking Up Big Business   87

9. A Foot in the Door   99

Notes   117

Index   129

Acknowledgments

I am happy to acknowledge the generous assistance I have received while writing this book. Originally, my study of corporate history and law was made possible by a post-doctoral research grant from the National Fellows Program at the Hoover Institution on War, Revolution and Peace. I owe special thanks to W. Glenn Campbell, the director of the Hoover Institution, for his continuing support and encouragement.

Several of my colleagues read a draft of the manuscript and offered me the benefit of their criticisms. They include Martin Anderson, Dennis L. Bark, Thomas Gale Moore, Gerald Musgrave, and Alvin Rabushka. Others who offered valuable suggestions include William C. Bark, James D. Cox, William B. Dawkins, Allan Gotthelf, Davis E. Keeler, David H. Rogers, and Kenneth E. Scott.

I am grateful to many earlier writers on business law and corporate history. In addition to those whose ideas and influence I acknowledge in the text, I must single out three for special mention: Professor Henry G. Manne, whose writings originally sparked my interest in corporations; the late Professor Adolf A. Berle, Jr., whose writings on the history of corporate law were a valuable source of factual support for my viewpoint; and Professor Alan R. Bromberg, whose excellent treatise on partnership law enabled me to identify the essential differences between partnership and corporations.

In addition, I want to acknowledge my intellectual indebtedness to Ayn Rand. However, I do not wish to imply that she—or anyone else named above—agrees with or endorses my analysis, interpretations, or conclusions.

My appreciation goes to Mickey Hamilton, general manager of the Hoover Institution Press, for her competence and concern. Thanks also are due to John Ziemer, editor; Rachelle Marshall, proofreader; and Anna Clarke, production coordinator.

As always, I owe the greatest thanks to my wife, Bea. She helped me at every stage with perceptive criticisms and suggestions.

ROBERT HESSEN

Stanford, California

Prologue

Giant corporations affect the life and livelihood of nearly everyone. Many people work for one or invest in several, and almost everyone consumes the products of dozens or even hundreds of others. Combining the capital of millions of investors and the talents of millions of workers, giant corporations are a testament to the ability of free men, motivated by self-interest, to engage in sustained, large-scale, peaceful cooperation for their mutual benefit and enrichment. As a result, Americans today enjoy a standard of living—of luxury, leisure, and longevity—that is unprecedented in world history and unparalleled in contemporary socialist societies.

Yet, despite the undeniable productive achievements of American business corporations, they are fiercely denounced. But they deserve to be defended. This book offers a defense and is addressed to every man and woman who has a stake in the survival and prosperity of corporations.

But, one might ask, why bother to defend the corporation, and against what? Chiefly, against the accusation that it is an illegitimate institution. This claim is made by writers of every political persuasion. Professor Irving Kristol commented that neither the Founding Fathers nor Adam Smith would understand or approve of the giant corporation as it exists today: "They would have asked themselves the same questions we have been asking ourselves for almost a century now: Who 'owns' this leviathan? Who governs it—and by what right, and according to what principles?" He adds that "the trouble with the large

corporation today is that it does not possess a clear theoretical—i.e., ideological—legitimacy" within the framework of capitalism.[1]
Similarly, Professor John Kenneth Galbraith wrote:

> The case for private ownership through equity capital disappears whenever the stockholder ceases to have power—when he or she or it becomes a purely passive recipient of income. The management is a self-governing, self-perpetuating bureaucracy. It can make no claim to the traditional immunity associated with property ownership. The logical course is for the state to replace the helpless stockholder as a supervisory and policy-setting body; the forthright way to accomplish this is to have a public holding company take over the common stock.[2]

Those familiar with the literature on corporate reform will recognize that the views of Kristol and Galbraith derived from *The Modern Corporation and Private Property*, by Adolf A. Berle, Jr. and Gardiner C. Means. Since its publication in 1932, it has been the single most influential work ever written about corporations, and one whose central thesis continues to dominate contemporary discussions of giant corporations.

Briefly, Berle and Means claimed that during the twentieth century the increase in the number of corporate shareholders, each owning only a few shares, has enabled corporate officers to usurp authority; the shareholders have lost control over their own wealth and the officers have gained control of wealth which they do not personally own. Because of this separation of ownership and control, giant corporations are no longer private property and do not deserve to be treated or protected as private property by the government.

Like many subsequent writers, Berle and Means invoked the authority of Adam Smith to prove that giant corporations are incompatible with capitalism and that they are not private property.[3] Adam Smith's defense of private property and capitalism (which he called "the system of natural liberty") was based on three assumptions about the typical business firm: that it would be small-scale, that the individual owner or small group of owners would invest personal savings in their business venture, and that they would manage it directly, reaping profits or suffering losses, depending on their own personal managerial abilities.

Those who invoke Adam Smith as a critic of corporations are really creating and demolishing a straw man. There is no justification for equating capitalism with a particular configuration of small firms run by their owners, and Adam Smith's preferences are not binding upon free men who prefer to create some other arrangement. The essence of capitalism is the inviolability of individual rights, including one's right to use or invest one's wealth as one chooses, and one's right to associate with others for any peaceful purpose and under any terms of association that are acceptable to all parties concerned.

The idea that giant corporations lack legitimacy because they are not private property must be analyzed and refuted. If this idea prevails, it will endanger whatever degree of autonomy today's giant corporations still possess. In answer to the questions: "Who 'owns' this new leviathan? Who governs it—and by what right, and according to what principles?" I will argue that the shareholders own it, that the officers make major decisions without consulting the owners, and that this relationship is unobjectionable because it rests on the principles of choice, consent, and contractual authorization.

Another equally influential idea—the concession theory— also needs to be challenged. The concession theory holds that every corporation, regardless of size, owes its existence to governmental permission, and that through its charter a corporation obtains certain special privileges, such as limited liability, which only government can confer. This view is reflected in Professor Willard F. Mueller's comment: "Most Americans seem to have forgotten that business corporations are created and survive only as a special privilege of the state," and in Professor Robert Dahl's observation:

> It is absurd to regard the corporation simply as an enterprise established for the sole purpose of allowing profit-making. One has simply to ask: Why should citizens, through *their* government, grant special rights, powers, privileges, and protections to any firm except on the understanding that its

activities are to fulfill *their* purposes? Corporations exist because we allow them to do so.[4]

The importance of the concession theory can hardly be
overstated. It is a tenet of orthodox legal theory, accepted as a
self-evident truth by people of all political persuasions. But those
who are hostile to corporations put it to special use. When critics
demand, for example, that Congress compel corporations to
adopt a new system of internal decision making, the obvious
question is why do the critics believe that government has any
right to regulate the internal affairs or dictate the internal
structure of private business. The reason they offer is that
corporations, unlike other organizations or associations, are
"creatures of the state" because they require governmental permission to exist. From this basic premise, they conclude that in
return for this permission, corporations must submit to whatever
constraints or demands government may choose to impose upon
them. But is this basic premise valid?
    In this book, the belief that corporations require govern-
mental permission to exist and that they are the recipients of
special privileges will be challenged. I will present an alternative
known as the "inherence theory"; i.e., corporations are created
and sustained entirely by an exercise of individual rights, specifically freedom of association and freedom of contract. The inherence theory was suggested by several earlier writers, including
Victor Morawetz, Frederick W. Maitland, Wesley Newcomb
Hohfeld, and Shaw Livermore, but none of them ever attempted
to present it systematically.
    The concession theory contains an important corollary: a
corporation is not an association of human beings but rather a
"fictitious legal person" or an "artificial legal entity" distinct from
its owners and officers. If a corporation is an artificial legal entity,
does it possess any rights? And should it be entitled to equal
protection under the Fourteenth Amendment: "No State shall
make or enforce any law which shall abridge the privileges and
immunities of citizens of the United States; nor shall any State
deprive any person of life, liberty, or property, without due
process of law; nor deny to any person within its jurisdiction the

equal protection of the law"? Some people are puzzled and others are angered that a fictitious legal person is accorded the same substantive and procedural safeguards that apply to individuals. But is it necessary to view a corporation as an artificial legal person? I will present an alternative view—a corporation is in fact an association of individuals who are entitled to the same rights and legal protections which apply to all other individuals and organizations.

But even if one grants that the Berle thesis and the concession theory are open to criticism, why bother to challenge these ideas now? The immediate occasion for writing this book is to respond to Ralph Nader's latest attack on corporations. What differentiates Nader's criticism of corporations is not his ideas, but the fact that his analysis is tied to specific "remedial" legislation. His proposal for federal chartering of corporations has been the subject of congressional hearings, and an act to embody his recommendations is being drafted for congressional consideration.

Briefly, Nader's bill of indictment runs as follows: Incorporation requires governmental permission or authorization, hence corporations are creatures of the state. The government bestows various privileges on corporations, such as limited liability, in return for a corporate promise to serve the public interest, but this promise is forgotten and never enforced. These special privileges give corporations an immense advantage in competition with noncorporate businesses, such as partnerships. Therefore, corporations are more likely to survive, to grow, and to reap profits. Once corporations attain giant size, they are indistinguishable from governments because they wield power of equal magnitude over their employees, customers, and neighboring communities; they are private governments, but undemocratic and despotic.

Furthermore, according to Nader (embracing the thesis of Berle and Means), as a corporation prospers, it attracts an increasing number of shareholders. Eventually they become so numerous that with each shareholder owning only a comparatively few shares, the officers usurp control. Thereafter, the officers can and do behave irresponsibly, exposing customers and employees to injury and death due to poorly designed products and hazardous working conditions. Giant corporations ruthlessly extinguish their smaller competitors and then use their monopoly power to shamelessly overcharge consumers. And even the shareholders do not benefit from this extortion because the officers deliberately withhold dividends from them.

Ralph Nader's hostility to corporations is well-known and long-standing. He began attacking individual companies and industries in 1965 and since then has been searching for a wholesale remedy for the alleged evils and abuses of giant corporations as a class. In 1971, he first announced that he had discovered the cure—federal chartering of corporations—and he published a preliminary prescription in 1973, but not until 1976 did he release his comprehensive remedy. He presented two versions. The first, *Constitutionalizing the Corporation*, was issued in January, 1976, in an effort to persuade the Democratic party to endorse federal chartering in its platform. Although Nader did not achieve that goal, he did attract national attention to his proposal, including endorsement by four senators and hearings before the Senate Commerce Committee. In September 1976, with only a few minor changes, the proposal was presented in the book *Taming the Giant Corporation*, by Ralph Nader, Mark Green, and Joel Seligman.[5]

What is federal chartering and what does Nader hope it will achieve? He proposes that Congress compel every American corporation with sales exceeding $250 million or employees numbering more than 10,000 to obtain a federal charter in addition to state incorporation papers. At present, 700 corporations exceed these figures. This federal charter would serve as a domestic passport entitling a corporation to engage in interstate commerce. If a federally chartered corporation violates any of the conditions or restrictions imposed on it by the federal government, then its passport will be revoked and its products outlawed in interstate commerce.

This remedial legislation is urgent and long overdue, Nader says, because giant corporations are guilty of victimizing their shareholders, customers, and smaller competitors. He lays the blame on several factors: the discretionary authority over shareholders' wealth that corporate officers wield, corporations' secret conduct of their affairs, and the immunity from competitive challenge due to the sheer size of the corporate giants.

His federal chartering proposal would compel giant corporations to make major changes in their structure and operating methods. His demands fall into three major categories. First, he seeks to strip corporate officers of their authority to make decisions; instead, every "fundamental transaction" would have to be approved first by a board of directors consisting entirely of outsiders and then by the shareholders voting by mail in special plebiscites. He also wants to deny giant corporations any right of privacy; instead, he calls for compulsory disclosure of information sought by consumers, competitors, and governmental agencies. And finally, he proposes to dismantle the giant corporations by imposing a stringent new test of monopoly power, which would automatically trigger an antitrust action against any corporation whose market share exceeds 12 percent.

I will examine each of Nader's major claims and proposed remedies, but I will not attempt to refute his many accusations against specific products, companies, or industries. The purpose of this book is *not* to defend the policies, products, and performance of all corporations or of any particular corporation. Rather, its purpose is to demonstrate the legitimacy of the corporate form—which means its compatibility with the principles of capitalism: individual rights, private property, freedom of contract, and voluntary peaceful cooperation.

However, even if a few of Nader's accusations against specific corporations are true and based upon reasonable criteria, there is still no justification for a verdict of collective guilt against all giant corporations. Corporations should not be absolved from any of the responsibilities or liabilities that apply to individuals or to other organizations, either business or nonbusiness. On the contrary, regardless of their size, corporations should be held to exactly the same standards of conduct and accountability that apply to everyone else—nothing less but also nothing more. Any attempt to label them indiscriminately as members of a criminal class is unfair and unjustified. When a particular corporation is accused of a specific crime, its guilt is a matter to be proven in a court of law, not to be assumed glibly and then used as a pretext for stigmatizing and punishing all corporations.

If Ralph Nader's attack on corporations goes unanswered, federal chartering may be enacted. If Congress accepts his blueprint, giant corporations would remain nominally private, but in actuality—in terms of the power to determine their own goals and operating methods—they would become subsidiaries of the federal government. If a truth-in-labelling law were applied to federal chartering, it would be identified as a de facto government expropriation of the largest American business enterprises. Surely, on a measure of such far-reaching importance, a debate, not a monologue, is needed.

Chapter 1

The Concession Theory of Corporations

"The corporation is, and must be, the creature of the State. Into its nostrils the State must breathe the breath of a fictitious life."[1] This statement accurately expressed Anglo-American legal theory until the mid-nineteenth century; government was thought to play a godlike role in the creation of corporations. In England, at first, only the king possessed this creative, life-bestowing power, but by the eighteenth century Parliament had also acquired it. After the American colonies won their independence from king and Parliament, the authority to create corporations was vested in the state legislatures. As the authors of the first American treatise on corporations declared in 1832: "The state, or commonwealth, stands in the place of the King."[2] The consent of the legislature was needed to create a corporation; to exercise corporate powers without a grant of legislative authority was considered to be an invasion of sovereign prerogative. Until the mid-nineteenth century, the process of incorporation was expensive and time-consuming because a special act of a state legislature was needed in order for a corporate venture to be legally valid.

However, during the nineteenth century, a revolutionary new method of creating corporations was adopted in both England and America. Under general incorporation statutes, governments no longer exercised life-creating powers. Today a group of individuals can create a corporation by drawing up a contract known as articles of incorporation. The articles need contain only certain basic information about the intended activities and initial financing of a new firm. The founders can incorporate in *any* state, regardless of the location of their principal manufacturing facilities or sales outlets, and the corporation is free to operate in any or all of the other states. After the founders select a state, they submit two copies of the articles to a designated state official, who cannot refuse to certify the copies if they contain the required information. From the moment the state official issues a certificate of incorporation, the articles become a legally enforceable contract, and the corporation exists in the eyes of the law.

This procedure hardly fits the description of government breathing the breath of life into a corporation. On the contrary, since the mid-nineteenth century, the creation of a corporation has been a standardized formality—a paperwork procedure open to nearly all would-be incorporators. Why, then, despite this fundamental change in procedure, does the older view of a corporation as a creature of the state still persist? And why is this anachronistic doctrine still being invoked by advocates of federal chartering? The answer to these questions lies in an examination of the origins of the concession theory.

The concession theory was a by-product of the Norman Conquest of England in 1066 A.D. When the Normans subjugated the people of the British isles, all existing titles to landownership were abrogated, and all land became the property of William the Conqueror. He, in turn, parceled out much of it to his lieutenants in return for pledges of continued loyalty and military support. In the Anglo-Norman system of feudalism, the king's subjects possessed no rights to liberty or property. Any wealth or land that a person was allowed to retain was considered to be a privilege or concession granted by the Crown, in return for which some compensation was demanded.

The kings of medieval England pursued a policy of systematic extortion. If any aspect of life escaped taxation, it was by oversight, not by design. In the words of Professor A. L. Poole, this system amounted to "blackmail on the part of the Crown against its subjects. In effect the king says: 'I will destroy you, seize your land and personal property unless you satisfy me with a payment.' "[3] Although often disguised as gifts or benevolences, these payments were compulsory; in exchange for these levies, the Crown offered protection against the local nobles, who were even more rapacious and insatiable in their financial demands than the Crown. The king thus shielded his subjects from his own lieutenants. The primary beneficiaries of this curious system of extortion were the boroughs, guilds, churches, and charities of medieval England. Each of these organizations was known as a corporation, although none was a corporation in the sense of being a private, profit-seeking business venture based on investment.

But *why* were these nonbusiness organizations called corporations, and why have they subsequently been widely regarded as the prototypes of business corporations?

The Borough as a Corporation

How did the borough, a form of municipal government, come to be classified as a corporation?

Medieval kings used the ancient system of tax farming as a means of raising revenues. The task of collecting taxes was delegated to tax farmers, private citizens who agreed to remit a fixed sum to the royal treasury in exchange for the right to keep any taxes collected above the specified amount. This system of tax farming placed an intolerable burden on merchants and tradesmen in the boroughs. They tried to reduce their taxes by petitioning the Crown for permission to tax themselves; their goal was to cut out the middleman, the tax farmer. If they could obtain this permission, the borough could remit a fixed sum to the Crown, an amount significantly smaller than that which the tax farmers normally extracted from them. The merchants sent petitions to the king, acting in their capacity as burgesses, that is, as citizens and freemen of the borough.[4]

Whenever the king acceded to such petitions, a royal charter would be issued to the burgesses of the borough, granting them specific privileges, such as self-assessment and exemption from certain tolls and taxes. But a problem arose when the original burgesses to whom the grant had been made died and were succeeded by others. Neither the Crown nor the succeeding burgesses wanted to return to the prior situation; so the practice gradually arose of treating the royal franchise—the charter confirming the borough's privilege of self-assessment—as a grant not merely to the specific group of burgesses who originally had petitioned for it but rather to them and to their successors *in perpetuity*. This, then, was the process by which the chartered boroughs of medieval England came to be classified as corporations, which Sir William Blackstone defined as "many persons united together in one society, and . . . kept up by a perpetual succession of members, so as to continue for ever."[5]

Medieval boroughs and modern business corporations share one minor characteristic, perpetual existence. Their differences are far more numerous and fundamental—most importantly, a corporation involves voluntary investment in a profit-oriented venture, while a borough is a unit of government. It is invalid to define a corporation as a group with continuity of existence despite changes in its membership. Such a sweeping definition would mean that nearly every group, organization, and society could be called a corporation. Even a family or an army or the human race itself would be a corporation—which they obviously are not. This definition, therefore, is superficial and misleading. The perpetual existence of the medieval borough does not make it a bona fide precursor of the business corporation; the fact that a borough was a creature of the state is irrelevant to discussions of modern business.

The Guild as a Corporate Precursor

The medieval guild also has been called a forerunner of the modern business corporation. Beyond the fact that both originated as voluntary associations, the similarities quickly fade. Originally the guilds were fraternal organizations of merchants or craftsmen in a particular line of commerce, but they soon ceased to be private associations. Throughout the twelfth and thirteenth centuries the guilds sought and were granted legal powers to enforce standardized prices and quality of products and to establish uniform hours and wages for their journeymen and apprentices.

Guild members wanted to eliminate every form of competitive rivalry—and they succeeded. A steady succession of guilds was granted royal charters giving them exclusive jurisdiction over their particular trades. Thereafter, when a guild issued rules and regulations, they were binding on everyone in that trade, not merely upon those who had agreed to join the guild and to obey its edicts. Anyone who ignored or defied the guild was subject to severe legal sanctions.[6]

A guild more closely resembled an agency of municipal

government than a voluntary business association; the guild was "the department of town administration whose duty it was to maintain and regulate the trade monopoly."[7] Professor Samuel Williston wrote that a guild's power differed from that of a municipal borough only in that "instead of having for its field all inhabitants of a district and local legislation of every character, the guild was confined to such inhabitants of the district as carried on a certain trade and to regulations suitable to that trade. So far as that trade was concerned, *the right of government* belonged to the guild."[8]

A guild was a corporation in the sense of possessing perpetual existence despite changes in membership, but it more closely resembled a borough, a unit of government, than it did a business corporation, a voluntary, private enterprise for profit. Medieval guilds truly were creatures of the state, but, again, this has no bearing upon business corporations created by contract centuries later.

The Medieval Church as Corporation

The third alleged precursor of the business corporation was the medieval church. The supposed link is the phenomenon known as the corporation sole, a concept created to keep church property out of the reach of English kings.

After the Norman Conquest, English bishops and abbots held their ecclesiastical lands in feudal tenure, and whenever an incumbent bishop or abbot died, legal title to the land escheated (i.e., reverted) to the king. In contrast, land owned by a noncleric reverted only if the owner died without heirs. But a cleric, by definition, could not have any legitimate heirs, and title reverted to the king. Hence it was necessary for a new bishop or abbot to compensate the king for returning the deceased cleric's lands to the church.

An option was open, however; ecclesiastic communities could have followed the example of boroughs and guilds by petitioning the Crown to designate them as corporations aggregate, that is, organizations with continuous existence despite changes in membership. But this option was unacceptable to the church hierarchy because the church rejected the notion that lower ecclesiastics—

priests and monks—shared authority with their superiors—
bishops and abbots.[9] Instead, the concept of corporation sole was
devised. The position of bishop or abbot was designated as a
perpetual office, legally independent of the particular person
who happened to be the officeholder at any given time. Thereafter, when a bishop or abbot died, ownership of church lands was
not interrupted.

Undeniably, the idea of corporation sole was a clever solution to this ecclesiastical dilemma, but it is irrelevant if one wishes
to understand the nature or origins of the business corporation.
Aside from the obvious differences in purpose, a business corporation involves simultaneous ownership by several persons (not a
succession of individual owners, who actually are trustees.)[10] The
creation of a corporation sole required royal permission; hence it
was a creature of the state. But, once again, the concession theory
is irrelevant to an understanding of modern business enterprise.

The Charitable Trust as a Corporation

The fourth type of medieval corporation was the trust, a
legal form used to create universities, hospitals, and charitable
institutions. A trust was classified as a corporation because it was
intended to have perpetual existence. The creator of a trust had
to obtain a royal charter because he was transferring legal title to
property into the hands of an on-going group—a board of
trustees—and thereby was denying the Crown revenues to which
it otherwise would have been "entitled" when the original property owner died. Creating a trust meant that there never would be
a break in the title of ownership because, as one or more trustees
died, the survivors would name successors to fill the vacancies.[11]

The Crown tolerated this loss of revenue because the objective of a trust was considered meritorious. However, the royal
charter always contained a clause reserving visitatorial rights for
the king; that is, he could appoint someone to verify that the trust
actually was carrying out the purpose specified by its creator and
sanctioned by the Crown. If the king's agent, the visitor, discovered that the trustees were not carrying out the authorized
purpose, the trust could be voided and the property either would
revert to the donor or his heirs or to the Crown.[12] This was pre-

cisely the issue at stake in the famous *Sutton's Hospital* case of 1613; namely, had a valid charitable trust been established and was it actually fulfilling its intended purpose.

When the Lord Chief Justice, Sir Edward Coke, rendered his opinion in this case, he offered the formulation that became the first authoritative expression of the concession theory of corporations: "A Corporation aggregate of many is invisible, immortal, & resteth only in intendment and consideration of the Law."[13] Coke's dictum was adopted not only by Sir William Blackstone in his *Commentaries on the Laws of England* (1765) but, more importantly, by Chief Justice John Marshall in the *Dartmouth College* case of 1819. Marshall merely paraphrased Coke, declaring that "a corporation is an artificial being, invisible, intangible, and existing only in contemplation of law."[14]

Nonetheless, these authoritative opinions really do not apply to business corporations because these opinions emanated from cases involving charitable trusts. Since a business corporation is not a trust—and certainly not a charitable trust—there is no basis to conclude that it is a creature of the state.

Evaluating the Concession Theory

The discussion of corporations in Blackstone's *Commentaries* did not refer to business enterprises. Years later, in 1793, when Stewart Kyd wrote the first major treatise on corporations, the term still did not denote a profit-oriented business. Yet the principles set forth by Blackstone and Kyd were later applied to business corporations by English and American judges who accepted the concession theory without examining how it had originated or whether it actually suited the facts. Why did the courts apply precedents from medieval institutions to business corporations created centuries later? The answer lies in the Anglo-American system of common law and its theory of precedents.

Common law refers to the body of procedural rules, substantive decisions, and legal theories that originated in medieval England and still is the basis of American judicial decisions today. The major premise of the common law system has traditionally been that judges do not *create* the law; instead, they *discover* it.

Their task is to seek out the rules applicable to each case by finding a custom or judicial precedent set forth by an earlier court. On the implied assumption that there are no unprecedented situations, every dispute is to be resolved by invoking some earlier decision.

When the first corporations (called joint-stock companies) were created in sixteenth-century England, they represented a new type of business organization and, as such, should have required the creation of new legal principles. Instead, the courts found precedents to apply to them by equating them with earlier corporations. As Professor Julius Goebel aptly observed:

> The English courts from Coke's day until long after the American Revolution are busy with boroughs, colleges, hospitals and ecclesiastical establishments; rarely do they have to deal with commercial corporations. Kyd's work on corporations (1793), the first comprehensive treatise, could as well have been written in 1600 for all the light it throws upon such questions as the rights of stockholders, limitations upon liability, or the internal set-up of business corporations. Here, if ever, have we an instance of a great social institution evolving unaided by contemporary judicial intervention. The courts, like Lot's wife, were looking backward; the merchants and capitalists were looking ahead.[15]

Because the medieval corporations have no relation to voluntary business activity or to investment for profit, judicial cases involving them created no valid precedents applicable to modern business corporations. However, even if medieval corporations actually had been business organizations, the concession theory still would not be valid today. The need to obtain permission from the king to exist and to function arose in the feudal system—when kings acquired their legitimacy through violent conquest, when they claimed that all land belonged to them, when they engaged in systematic extortion of their subjects, when they maintained that associations for peaceful purposes could not be formed without paying protection money, and when any exercise of freedom of association or freedom of contract was construed as an invasion of the king's unlimited prerogative to control everyone and everything within his domain.

The concession theory arose in an era of royal absolutism; it is totally irrelevant to the modern view of a constitutional republic in which the head of state is an elected servant, not an omnipotent master, and in which the sphere of government is narrowly defined and circumscribed in the constitutions of nations and states and in the charters of cities, towns, and villages. It is ironic indeed that critics today seek to make corporations subservient by appealing to a theory created centuries ago to justify acts of extortion by absolute monarchs. As an argument for federal chartering, the concession theory is logically invalid and, above all, philosophically incompatible with a free society.

Chapter 2

Are Corporations Creatures of the State?

Ralph Nader shares the widely held belief that every corporation, through its charter, receives special privileges from the government and thus is a creature of the state. He has made this claim in print on at least seven different occasions, but his only proof consists of naming three corporate features—entity status, perpetual life, and limited liability—which he regards as state-created privileges.[1] Before challenging his claim, it will be useful to supply the explanations he does not provide.

One could make a case to support the idea that corporations receive special privileges from government only by showing that corporations possess features that other types of business organizations (such as partnerships) do not possess and that these features cannot be acquired by contractual agreement.

Nader and other critics believe that entity status is one such privilege. A corporation can sue and be sued in its own name, but a partnership cannot; unless authorized by law, a partnership can sue only in the name of its individual owners. The reason for this difference is that a partnership, in Anglo-American legal theory, is considered to be an *aggregate*, an association of individuals acting together to pursue a common business objective. In contrast, a corporation is held to be something entirely different: an *entity*, a fictitious legal person, an artificial legal being, which exists independently of its individual owners. The legal right of a corporation to sue in its own name is an immense convenience resulting from the fact that the law views a corporation as a distinct entity. Presumably, this point supports Nader's belief that entity status is a state-created privilege.

Perpetual life has also been suggested as a special privilege. A partnership is automatically dissolved whenever one of the general partners dies, goes bankrupt, becomes insane, is expelled, or wishes to withdraw. Terms like transient, ephemeral, and short-lived are often used to describe partnerships. In contrast, a corporation is called immortal or eternal because, as a distinct entity, it continues to exist despite changes in the ranks of its owners and because the law permits the founders of a corporation to specify perpetual duration in the articles of incorporation. Thus, immortality also seems to be a privilege conferred by the state.

Limited liability has also been claimed as a special privilege of corporations. Partners (like sole proprietors) incur unlimited personal liability for business debts. If the assets of the partnership are insufficient to settle the claims of creditors, then the total personal property of each partner is subject to seizure for the benefit of creditors. But the shareholders of a corporation possess *limited* liability, and if a corporation cannot meet its debt obligations to outside creditors, the shareholders cannot be assessed to make up the deficit. A shareholder incurs no liability beyond the amount that he has chosen to invest because the law holds that a corporation is an entity distinct from the shareholders and that it contracts debts in its own name. Hence, by law, the owners are not responsible for the corporation's debts.[2]

These three fundamental differences between partnerships and corporations appear to prove that a corporation is a recipient of special privileges bestowed by government. And in exchange, say corporate critics like Nader, corporations should be subject to special restrictions and controls. If the special privileges theory is invalid, then so is Nader's corollary.

Corporate Features by Contract

Can entity status, perpetual duration, and limited liability be explained by the inherence theory, that is, as being contractual?

Entity status merely means that a corporation can sue (and be sued) as a unit, instead of having to specify the name of every shareholder. It also means that a corporation can hold legal title to property despite changes in the ranks of its shareholders. If a privilege means a favor or immunity bestowed by law on one party at the expense of another, then entity status cannot be classified as a privilege. Professor Adolf A. Berle wrote: "More accurately, the associates are granted a legal convenience, in that they may use the courts without writing the name of every shareholder into their papers." If this convenience is considered a privilege, then it is neutralized, for as Berle noted, "The reverse process—that of liability to be sued under a single name, is manifestly not advantageous to them, but is rather a measure of fairness to their opponents."[3]

Moreover, entity status is an optional feature available to all unincorporated businesses, including partnerships, limited partnerships, and trusts. Owners can designate trustees to represent them in lawsuits and to accept or convey title to property on their behalf. Being a legal entity, then, is clearly not a feature unique to corporations, or a one-sided advantage, or a state-created privilege.

Nor is it accurate to call perpetual duration a special privilege conferred by government. Perpetual duration simply means that the articles of incorporation need not be renewed, unless the founders originally specified that the enterprise was to exist only for a fixed period of time. The privilege of perpetuity certainly does not guarantee that a corporation will continue in business forever; more than half of all corporate ventures fail and cease to exist within five years of their inception. On the other hand, although partnerships are not automatically immortal, many firms—of attorneys, accountants, architects, and stockbrokers, to mention a few—have been in continuous existence for a century or more.

If they choose to do so, partners can make their enterprise immortal by adopting a continuity agreement specifying that the firm will not be liquidated when one of the general partners dies or withdraws. After outlining a variety of means by which partners can assure the continuity of their enterprise, Professor Alan R. Bromberg, a leading authority on partnership law, writes: "By skillful use of agreements, partnerships can be given virtually any desired degree of continuity."[4] The idea that government makes corporations immortal while partnerships cannot achieve a permanent, on-going existence is an illusion.

Limited liability is the most controversial and least understood corporate feature. How can it be explained except as a state-created privilege?

Limited liability actually is the result of an implied contract between the corporate owners and their creditors. As Professor Berle observed: "A clause could be put in every contract by which the apposite party [i.e., the creditor] limited his right of recovery to the common fund: the incorporation act may fairly be construed as legislating into all corporate contracts an implied clause to that effect."[5]

Contrary to popular belief, limited liability does not discriminate against creditors to the benefit of shareholders. Creditors cannot be compelled to accept a limited liability arrangement. They can, and often do, insist that one or more of the shareholders become personal guarantors or sureties for the debt. This fact explains why limited liability is often an illusory feature for a new or unstable corporate enterprise.[6] When creditors do accept limited liability, they do so, as Professor Berle noted, by means of an implied contract. Because creditors have a choice in the matter, limited liability cannot be viewed as a state-created privilege that benefits the corporation at the expense of the creditor.

Limited Liability for Torts

Thus far, the inherence theory—the idea that corporate features are created by contract—has been applied to entity status, perpetual duration, and limited liability for debts. But how can limited liability for torts be explained by a contractual theory, since tort victims do not consent to limit their claims to the assets of the corporation? Surely, limited liability for torts would seem to be a state-created privilege.

A tort is a wrong or injury (except breach of contract) for which the law awards compensation to the victim. Broadly, there are two major classifications: torts which are intentional—acts which are committed with deliberate malice, such as assault—and torts which are negligent or unintentional—acts which are accidental and unforeseen, resulting from oversight, carelessness, or failure to take adequate precautions. Most torts involving business firms are negligent rather than intentional. A classic example is an injury to a pedestrian caused by a vehicle owned by a business firm and operated by its employee or agent. In terms of liability, there is a crucial difference between a corporation and a partnership.

In legal language, the liability of partners for torts is joint and several. A tort victim may bring suit against the assets of the partnership, or against any one or combination of the partners, or against the firm and its members simultaneously, at his option.[7] A partner is liable to the extent of his *total* wealth, not merely the amount he has invested in the partnership, for claims by tort victims. If only one of the partners is sued, he must pay the full amount of the settlement (unless, of course, it exceeds his total wealth), and then he can try to recover the amount from the assets of the partnership or from the other partners personally.

In contrast, a shareholder's liability for torts is limited to his investment in the corporation, and he cannot be singled out to pay the whole amount (unless, of course, he personally committed the tortious act). If a vehicle owned by a corporation and operated by one of its employees or agents injures a pedestrian and if the damages exceed the assets of that corporation, then shareholders are not personally liable, either individually or collectively, and they cannot be assessed to make up the deficit.

The customary rationale for this rule is that a corporation is an entity distinct from its shareholders so "they" are not responsible for the torts committed by "it" or its agents and employees. Thus, it seems that shareholders' limited liability for torts is a privilege, shielding them from liability, conferred by government and never created by contract.

How, if at all, can limited liability for torts be integrated into a *contractual* theory of corporations? The answer is that it can't— and it needn't be. The question poses a false alternative: either limited liability for torts is a state-created privilege or it is contractual (which it obviously is not). In fact, there is a third possibility.

The rules of tort liability orginated many centuries ago in England when courts established the doctrine of *respondeat superior*—let the master be answerable for the acts of his servant. This principle of vicarious liability is based on the premise that the servant commits the tort while engaged in some activity on behalf of the master (for example, he injures a pedestrian while driving the master's carriage) and that the servant is personally hired, instructed, and supervised by the master. By holding a master fully liable for the torts committed by his servants, the courts gave the tort victim someone solvent ("a deep pocket") to sue for damages. But, equally important, the courts were serving notice upon masters that they must carefully choose and closely supervise their servants or else bear the financial consequences of their neglect to do so.[8]

Subsequently, application of the principle of vicarious liability was extended to sole proprietors and to general partners on the premise that they personally select and monitor their employees and agents. This extension is reasonable, but it does not automatically follow that the same principle should be extended to corporate shareholders. Vicarious liability should only apply to those shareholders who play an active role in managing an enterprise or in selecting and supervising its employees and agents. The tort liability of inactive shareholders should be the same as that of limited partners—that is, limited to the amount invested—and for the same reason; namely, inactive shareholders and limited partners contribute capital but do not participate actively in management and control.

The proper principle of liability should be that whoever controls a business, *regardless of its legal form*, should be personally liable for the torts of agents and employees. Thus, in partnerships, vicarious liability would fall upon the general partners only, while in corporations, the officers would be liable (whether they are owner-investors or hired managers). The safeguards open to general partners and corporate officers would include more careful selection and closer supervision of personnel and the purchase of larger amounts of liability insurance.

The current rule that shareholders are not personally liable for corporate torts because "it" is an entity distinct from "them" has permitted and condoned an injustice: the use of the so-called one-man corporation and the close corporation. Instead of buying enough liability insurance to cover potential tort claims, a sole proprietor forms a one-man corporation, and then it (deliberately undercapitalized and underinsured) rather than he, the active decision-maker, is liable to tort victims for the acts of its employees and agents. Similarly, the entity doctrine enables general partners to limit their tort liability by forming a close corporation and then by mutual consent to discard nearly every other corporate feature. The use of one-man and close corporations has unfairly thrust the burden of accidents and injuries upon the hapless victims. It is an abuse long-noted and vigorously condemned in legal literature, but one which is inevitable and ineradicable as long as the idea persists that a corporation is legally a distinct entity.

Two qualifications should be noted. First, tort victims do not necessarily benefit from the rule that general partners bear unlimited liability. In fact, there is no guarantee that a tort victim will collect anything—that depends on whether the partnership carries liability insurance and whether the partners possess any assets. If the net assets of the partners (individually or collectively) are meager or nonexistent, there is no one to pay the tort victim's claim for damages.

Second, the rule that each partner bears unlimited liability for torts may actually produce an effect opposite of that intended. The source of the problem is that, by law, tort liability is joint and several—one partner may be singled out to pay the whole amount. A partner who may be willing to pay his *proportional* share may, understandably, be unwilling to pay the whole amount. And he may feel that the courts should distinguish between intentional and unintentional torts. Liability for an intentional tort should be imposed only on the individual partner who committed or authorized the act, while liability for unintentional torts should be joint only; that is, it should fall proportionally on all partners. But American judges not only view debt liability and tort liability identically, they also refuse to differentiate between intentional and unintentional torts. Thus, this judicial tradition may be detrimental to tort victims because it encourages individuals with substantial assets to form close corporations in order to limit their liability for torts.

Regardless of one's view about limited liability for torts, the whole issue is irrelevant to giant corporations, which either carry substantial liability insurance or possess sizable net assets from which claims can be paid.

The Entity Idea

In America the source of the idea that a corporation is a distinct entity was Chief Justice John Marshall's 1819 dictum that "a corporation is an artificial being, invisible, intangible, and existing only in contemplation of law."[9] His statement still serves as the leading definition of a corporation and is widely quoted in judicial opinions. Nonetheless, Marshall's definition is defective because it fails to differentiate a corporation from a partnership. And it is confusing because it is metaphorical, not literal (as a definition should be); it makes a corporation sound like a hallucination—a legal pink elephant. But Ralph Nader believes that John Marshall's definition cannot be improved because it "still best expresses the idea that corporations are not endowed by their creator [i.e., government] with any inalienable rights."[10]

Other writers who do not share Nader's animus against corporations have attempted to reformulate Marshall's definition into nonmetaphorical language. One recent attempt states: "A corporation . . . is a fictitious legal person . . . In the eyes of the law, therefore, the group has an existence which is independent of its individual members."[11] Another scholar, after surveying numerous attempts to revise Marshall's definition, reports that they all are "pervaded by the notion of a 'body' or an 'entity' or an 'artificial legal creation,' the continuance of which does not depend on that of the component persons, and the being or existence of which is owed to an act of state."[12]

But the entity concept serves no valid purpose. Like the idea that corporations are creatures of the state, it is a vestige of medieval mentality and should be discarded. The proper alternative is the inherence theory of corporations—the idea that men have a natural right to form a corporation by contract for their own benefit, welfare, and mutual self-interest. It is the only theory of corporations that is faithful to the facts and philosophically consistent with the moral and legal principles of a free society.

Chapter 3

What is a Corporate Charter?

In his 1976 book *Taming the Giant Corporation*, Ralph Nader did not discuss what a corporate charter is, what it says, or what purpose it serves—a curious omission in a work proposing a new system of chartering. On an earlier occasion, however, he did offer his view of the charter. Writing in 1973, he said: "In order to exist it [a corporation] must obtain a charter. A corporate charter is in effect an agreement whereby a government gives the corporate entity existence and that entity, in return, agrees to serve the public interest."[1]

What Nader calls a charter is actually the articles of incorporation, which have nothing to do with state permission and privileges or any corporate promises to serve the public interest—a term that is central to his thesis but nowhere defined in any of his writings. The articles actually contain certain purely factual information: the name of the business; the intended duration (which may be a specified number of years rather than perpetual); the purpose of the business; the number of shares to be issued and the voting rights of shareholders if more than one class of stock is to be created; the amount of capital to be paid in before the business commences; the name of the registered agent; the number and identity of the first group of directors; and the names of the three or more incorporators. Nothing else is required in the articles.

When this information is presented to the secretary of state (or department of corporations) in the state in which the incorporators choose to establish the legal residence of their enterprise, the state official has no discretionary powers. He cannot demand any additional information; he cannot extract any oath of corporate allegiance to the public interest; he cannot even refuse to certify the corporate charter. He must sign and date both copies, keeping one on file in his office, and he must issue a receipt (certificate of incorporation) attesting that the articles of incorporation have been filed.[2]

The state does *not* give life or birth to a corporation. Just as a registrar of deeds records every sale of land, and a county clerk records the birth of every baby, a commissioner of corporations records the formation of every corporation—*nothing more*. The function of a state—to record the creation of a corporation—is not essential to its existence, any more than a registrar of births is essential to the conception or birth of a child.

However, because a procedural requirement is involved—filing the articles with a state official—Nader equates this with state creation. But procedural requirements are not unique to corporations. On the contrary, procedural requirements apply to virtually all contracts. For example, to be legally valid, a marriage contract must follow specified procedural requirements: it must be performed by someone authorized by the state, it must be witnessed, and a signed certificate must be filed with the state. If these requirements make the state a party to a contract, then every marriage must be a *ménage à trois*—bride, groom, and government. Quite literally, the government plays a smaller role in the creation of a corporation than of a marriage. Yet who, for that reason, would describe a marriage as a creature of the state, or claim that a marriage certificate contains a promise to serve the public interest?

The Original Meaning of Charters

A legal scholar recently noted: "In the literal sense, no 'charter' is now issued to a business corporation under the general incorporation laws."[3] Nader's devotion to this anachronistic concept undoubtedly reflects his nostalgia for an obsolete political philosophy. His idea that a charter contains a promise to serve the state is a carryover from the sixteenth and seventeenth centuries, when the Tudor and Stuart monarchs reigned in England. Englishmen who wanted to travel or trade overseas had to obtain a charter—a royal permit—which the king would grant only if he stood to reap some gain. Freedom of commerce—freedom to join with others to engage in overseas trade—was viewed as a privilege or concession that the king could grant or withhold at will. When men sought the king's permission, their petitions contained glowing promises to serve the king, to bring wealth and glory to his realm.

Englishmen acting without obtaining a royal charter were subject to prosecution for usurping the sovereign's prerogative, a crime which carried the penalty of imprisonment and forfeiture of property. In an age when the divine right of kings was the prevailing political doctrine, men wisely avoided provoking the king's wrath. As a British legal historian observed:

> If they wished to trade overseas, to depart from the Realm, to take out ships and men, goods and bullion, it was as well to have the royal permission in writing. . . . Not only would a royal charter be a mark of royal favor and protection, but it would sanction something which the Crown would otherwise regard with jealousy and suspicion.[4]

In other words, men found it expedient to justify their request for charters in terms of benefit to the king so that he would not take offense at their exercise of commercial freedom. Any other course of action was inconceivable because the Tudors and Stuarts did not recognize the principles of individual rights or freedom of association.

Three centuries later, neither does Ralph Nader. He claims that all property rights are created by government: "The law creates and protects that bundle of rights called property or the corporation, and this same law can rearrange that bundle of rights if it is in the public interest." If the government does decide to modify or even abolish the right to private property, Nader says that no one should resist or complain: "It hardly seems valid to condemn the government for legally rearranging this bundle of rights when it created them in the first place."[5]

Nader's viewpoint is incompatible with the philosophy of a constitutional republic. Instead of holding that government is the protector of man's inalienable rights, he believes that government is the creator of rights, which it can revoke at will. His persistent use of the vague and rubbery phrase "the public interest" serves the same purpose as the theory of the divine right of kings—to justify the government's exercise of arbitrary and unlimited powers.

The Glorious Revolution of 1688, which ousted King James II, also repudiated the divine right of kings, and the American Revolution of 1776 sealed the doom of that medieval doctrine. Nonetheless, the concession theory of corporations survived, as did the medieval concept of a charter, by taking on a new purpose. Originally, a concession meant a grant of some benefit or privilege by government—as evidenced by a royal charter—in return for services rendered or to be rendered to the Crown. Kings bestowed two different kinds of favors: some people simply were permitted freedom of commerce without royal interference, while others were awarded exclusive monopolies to produce or import and to sell essential commodities (such as salt) or luxuries (such as silk). No distinction was made between these two types of concessions; both were regarded as diminishing the prerogatives of the sovereign ruler, and all recipients had to contribute funds to the king in exchange for a royal charter.[6]

In the late eighteenth century, after the American Revolution, concessions and charters acquired a new purpose. They signified an exclusive grant to construct, operate, and profit by an activity such as building a canal, bridge, wharf, or harbor, or organizing a bank or a water, fire, or street improvement company. The rationale for these grants was not to enrich royal favorites but to encourage the investment of private funds to supply quasi-governmental services. Businessmen, who otherwise would have formed a partnership, incurred the expense of obtaining a corporate charter from a state legislature. The charter gave them privileges and benefits that were granted only to corporations. These included a legally enforced monopoly, exemption from taxation, release of employees from militia and jury duty, power to exercise eminent domain, and authorization to hold lotteries as a means of raising capital.[7] Corporations in that era, as Professor Stuart Bruchey has observed, "were accorded certain exclusive privileges in order to encourage the devotion of scarce private capital to public ends."[8] These concessions were awarded for the same purpose as protective tariffs, that is, to encourage infant industries, specifically those supplying public services traditionally regarded as exclusive prerogatives of government.

Whether these chartered monopolies were necessary is certainly debatable, but whether they were popular is not. They were denounced as oppressive and exploitative. The fiercest critics were the Jacksonian reformers, men like William Leggett, Theodore Sedgwick, John Vethake, and William Gouge. They called for the abolition of all legally protected monopolies and special privileges—and their viewpoint eventually triumphed. Until that time, however, a corporation actually was a creature of the state.

The Advent of General Incorporation Laws

A new era began in 1837 when Connecticut passed the first all-purpose general incorporation statute. (Similar laws, such as New York's in 1811, had applied only to companies in specific industries.) The Act of 1837 established a standardized, simplified procedure for creating a corporation, one which other states copied in later decades. Instead of obtaining a special charter from the state legislature, the promoters of a corporation merely had to file certain information with an official of the state government. In response to decades of anticorporate criticism, the opportunity to incorporate was opened to nearly every group of would-be business associates.[9]

The state legislators really had no other choice. Once the force of public opinion made it impossible for them to continue awarding special privileges and monopolies, there was no reason for businessmen to seek state charters of incorporation. The legislators came to realize what businessmen already knew—that corporate features could be acquired without incorporation. British businessmen had made this discovery in the late seventeenth century; they simply copied the structure of the companies which held royal or parliamentary charters of incorporation. This enabled them, by contract and without obtaining governmental permission, to create joint-stock associations that offered investors the attraction of freely transferable shares. However, in 1720, at the urging of one of the chartered corporations, the South Sea Company, which resented the competition for investors' capital, Parliament passed the Bubble Act. This forbade companies without charters from issuing transferable shares or otherwise imitating corporate features.

But the measure backfired; businessmen and barristers soon devised a second way of acquiring corporate features without obtaining a charter from Parliament or the Crown. They did so by combining two long-established forms, the partnership and the trust. By designating a few of the potentially numerous partners as trustees for all the others and giving them exclusive authority to make contracts with outside parties, they concentrated managerial power in a few hands. Consequently, all other investors could be offered freely transferable partnership interests (virtually identical to corporate shares). The success of these unincorporated associations forced Parliament to relent, and in 1844 a highly permissive or enabling act was passed.[10]

An identical process occurred in America. Although the Bubble Act was extended to the American colonies in 1741, it had no impact. Like their British counterparts, American businessmen were able to create corporate features without incorporating. This enabled them to attract millions of dollars from investors for large-scale, long-term enterprises, such as textile factories and land development companies.[11]

The commonly held view that today's corporations are descendants of chartered corporations was challenged by Professor Shaw Livermore:

> It seems to be little realized that unincorporated private business associations of the eighteenth century, although barred from the legal status of corporations, approximated the business status and character of the modern corporation, both in England and in this country. . . . These business units, and not the old chartered bodies of the sixteenth and seventeenth centuries, are thus *the direct progenitors of the business corporation of today, which is formed as they were by private initiative and possesses a purely perfunctory and automatic legal approval.*[12]

A Revolutionary Transformation

Under the general incorporation statutes, corporations were no longer awarded special privileges or legally enforced monopolies. Thus, they ceased to be creatures of the state.

For nearly a century, legal scholars have recognized this fundamental change in the method and purpose of forming corporations. They have noted that the concession theory is now an anachronism, as is the idea that a corporation is awarded a charter in exchange for a promise to serve the state. In 1900, for example, Frederick W. Maitland, England's greatest legal historian, wrote:

> It has become difficult to maintain that the state makes corporations in any other sense than that in which the state makes marriages when it declares that people who want to marry can do so by going, and cannot do so without going, to church or registry. The age of corporations created by way of "privilege" is passing away.[13]

Similarly, in 1908, a leading American lawyer, Arthur W. Machen, Jr., noted:

> Always should the fact be recognized that nowadays when the right to organize a corporation is almost as free as the right to execute a deed of real estate, corporations are very different things from what they were when that right was confined to a few favorites of king or parliament.[14]

And in 1930, Professor Adolf A. Berle observed how much the concept of incorporation had changed but how little the change had been integrated into legal theory:

> So large a part of the legal history of corporations was bound up with actual cases in which the state had granted something—a charter plus a privilege, as monopolies to trade, the right to run a ferry, the right to mine gold, etc.,—that the legal concepts are still filled with survivals of the idea.[15]

A decisive change had occurred, Berle noted, "from the time when a corporation really did represent a bargain between a group of people and the state to the time when the state merely granted permission to a group of people to make an *agreement between themselves*."[16]

In 1948, Professor Berle began another of his books by stressing the total obsolescence of the idea that a charter is a grant of special privileges:

> Though the theory has not been seriously overhauled, the hundred years of corporate development from the middle of the 19th to the 20th Century has revolutionized the nature and content of corporate creation. . . . The economic fact is that a corporate charter is an agreement under which associates can invest their money and act as a group in an enterprise and along lines which they themselves or their predecessors devised and accepted.[17]

Why, then, a century later, is a corporation still referred to as a creature of the state—not only by Nader but even by those who are not hostile to corporations? There appear to be three reasons. To Nader, the appeal of the charter idea and the concession theory is that it harkens back to an era when individual liberty and freedom of commerce were privileges tied to serving "the public interest." For others, allegiance to the theory may simply represent intellectual inertia, a failure to reexamine and reformulate theory to make it correspond to reality.

But the third reason is one which applies alike to corporate admirers and adversaries. It is the failure to recognize that *all* business methods and relationships originate in the marketplace. Every tool of trade, from primitive barter to the most sophisticated new techniques, was created by private action. These include money (coins and currency), promissory notes, letters of credit, bills of exchange, stocks, bonds, checks, and credit cards. Similarly, all varieties of business organization—partnerships, limited partnerships, trusts, and corporations—were created and perfected in the marketplace through a process of experimentation. The reason is clear: because no one can be compelled to invest in a business or extend credit to it, the terms of association and the rules of liability have to be mutually acceptable to all parties— investors and creditors alike. None of these organizational forms was created by the decree of any king, court, or legislature.

Yet it cannot be denied that the courts and legislatures provide two valuable services that enhance the use of new organizational forms. They standardize the rules and procedures by which individuals create new enterprises and, thereafter, when an unanticipated problem or disagreement arises—either among the owners of the enterprise or between them and their outside creditors—the courts supply a solution which reflects as closely as possible the implicit intent of the parties to the dispute.

However, the claim that corporations are created by government contains the same logical error as the declaration that because the government is the *enforcer* of contracts, it is really their *creator*. When applied to corporations, the error consists of saying that because there are laws and judicial decisions pertaining to corporations, corporations are created by legislators and judges. On that premise, everything protected by law is a creature of the state unless there is no government at all. But this presents a false alternative: either statism or anarchism. Far from playing no role in relation to corporations, government performs a crucial role. But it is the role of *protector,* not creator.

Chapter 4

The Partnership-Corporation Continuum

Those who create a corporation must observe various state-prescribed formalities, while a partnership can be created entirely by private contract without notifying the state. Thus it seems that partnerships and corporations are polar opposites. But are they really? The answer to this question requires an understanding of how a corporation differs from a partnership and of what role government plays in their creation. This, in turn, requires a brief review of the features of partnerships.

Partnership is the oldest form of business co-ownership; it developed across many centuries of experimentation in the marketplace as businessmen tried to discover features that not only were agreeable to them as co-owners but also acceptable to their creditors. Partnership rests upon two assumptions. The first is that the partners collectively manage the business; therefore, unless otherwise agreed, each partner is entitled to an equal voice and an equal vote in decision making. The second is that every partner is a full-time, active participant in the business; therefore, unless otherwise agreed, they owe each other exclusive allegiance, and no one can simultaneously be a general partner in two firms, even if the firms are not competitors.

From the standpoint of creditors, the distinctive feature of partnership is that every partner is presumed to possess the powers and incur the obligations of a sole proprietor. (In fact, an early name for partnership was coproprietorship.) Every partner is presumed to be an authorized agent of the firm (that is, able to sign contracts binding on all the partners), and each partner is personally liable for the total debt obligations of the firm. These features undoubtedly originated at the insistence of creditors; instead of having to sue every partner so that each one would pay his share of the debt, creditors preferred that each partner act as a personal guarantor or surety for the total debt. Similarly, creditors wanted to be certain that a contract signed by a partner—and the resulting debt obligation—could not be subsequently repudiated by the other partners.

The fact that partners are mutual agents makes it necessary to restrict the transferability of partnership interests. If a partner could sell or give his interest to anyone, the other partners would be exposed to great risk; the new partner would have the power to sign contracts on behalf of everyone else. Clearly, partnership is a relationship ill-suited to strangers or to persons who harbor doubts about each other's intelligence, integrity, and ability. As a safeguard, therefore, every partner has the right to veto the admission of any proposed new partner; this right is known as *delectus personae*—the right to choose one's associates.

Partners are at liberty to modify these automatic features. For example, on *internal* matters, they can agree to give some of the partners an extra share of the profits or additional votes. They also can alter their *external* arrangements. For example, by withdrawing mutual agency powers from all but one of the partners, they can make him the managing partner and give him exclusive authority to enter into contracts with outsiders. Whatever changes the partners may decide to make, they are under no obligation to inform any governmental agency. In fact, they need not notify anyone of internal changes; whatever they decide among themselves can be kept strictly confidential. However, external changes—those altering the agency powers of partners—require notification to outsiders; none of the changes is binding upon creditors until and unless they receive notification. Even so, notification can be given through private messages, and no one is obliged to inform any state agency or obtain its approval.

Why, then, does an entirely different procedure apply to corporations? Why can't they be created without conforming to procedures prescribed by the state?

Statutory Requirements for Incorporation

Recall that the articles of incorporation contain purely factual information: the name of the business; its purpose and duration; number of shares and their voting rights; the amount of paid-in capital; the names of the registered agent, the incorporators, and the first group of directors. If the purpose of filing this information were to notify or protect the insiders—shareholders, directors, and officers—then it could be kept strictly confidential. But that is not the purpose. The filing requirement is designed as a safeguard for outsiders, such as creditors.

The crucial point is that unless notified to the contrary, outsiders are entitled to presume that they are dealing with a partnership. In the words of Professor Bromberg, partnership "is the residual form of business association, the one that is created when two or more persons join together to do business but do not take the trouble to adopt any other form."[1] Given that presumption, potential creditors must be advised that they are dealing with a corporation, which involves different rules of agency authority and financial liability. And that is precisely the reason for the legal requirements that a corporation file its articles with a state agency and that it use a symbol—Inc. or Corp.—after its name. Fulfilling these two requirements gives warning—constructive notice—to outsiders that they are not dealing with a partnership.

From the standpoint of creditors, there are two major differences in dealing with a corporation rather than with a partnership. First, shareholders, unlike partners, are not personal guarantors; that is, they do not accept unlimited personal liability for the firm's debts. Second, unlike partners, shareholders are not mutual agents; instead, agency powers are concentrated in the board of directors who in turn delegate these powers to an executive committee or to officers, such as the corporate president.[2] Neither the directors nor the officers intend to act as principals; rather, they are agents authorized to bind their principals—the shareholders collectively—up to the limit that they invested. As a safeguard, creditors must be able to trace the agency authority of the officers back to a source whose validity and legitimacy cannot be denied. The articles of incorporation serve that purpose; they identify the chain of authority from shareholders to directors to officers.

But why must the articles of incorporation be filed with a state agency? Why can't outsiders be notified directly that they are dealing with a firm whose owners are not mutual agents and accept only limited liability? In fact, it is possible to do this; a firm can acquire corporate features without becoming a corporation legally. However, the procedure for filing corporate articles with a state agency is a safe and simple substitute for explicit contracts and direct notification to outsiders. The purpose and benefit of this method of constructive notification is to reduce the need for individual notices and written contracts. In the lexicon of economics, it is an example of economizing on transaction costs, but it is not a justification for calling corporations creatures of the state.

One possible rejoinder to this argument would be to claim that *all* business organizations are state-created. After all, as a result of centuries of judicial decisions and legislative codifications, the features of partnership are so well established and clearly defined that it is possible to form a partnership without signing a written contract—a mere handshake or verbal agreement suffices. And even if a written partnership agreement is signed, it would be void unless contracts were enforceable in courts of law. Would anyone, for these reasons, call partnerships creatures of the state? The only premise on which one could do so is to assume that the norm is a government which does nothing except collect taxes and that everything else—police protection, contract enforcement, property safeguards—is a gift from government to its citizens. It is difficult to imagine a premise more inimical to the rights of man or more destructive of freedom of commerce and freedom of association.

Does a Corporation Possess Rights?

Far from being polar opposites, corporations and partnerships are members of the same family or genus; both are voluntary associations created by contract to conduct business for profit. In a free society, individuals have a right to pursue their goals and values either alone or in cooperation with others. Their exercise of freedom of action and freedom of association does not need to be justified in terms of benefits to anyone else. The right of individuals, alone or in groups, to exist and to function freely should be inviolate, subject to the moral and legal requirement that each in turn must recognize the rights of others. When individuals join together in a voluntary venture, they neither gain nor lose any rights. Regardless of the legal form they choose for their organization—a corporation or a partnership, for example—it can only acquire and exercise those rights which its members possess as individuals—nothing more and nothing less. The rights of any organization or association, including corporations, are the rights it derives from the individuals who create and sustain it.[3]

Although it may seem self-evident that a corporation derives its rights from its members in precisely the same way that a partnership draws its rights from its members, this contradicts a central tenet of Anglo-American legal theory. A partnership is held to be an *aggregate*, an association of individuals acting together to pursue a common goal, but a corporation is viewed as an *entity* or fictitious legal person that exists independently of its individual members. A major corollary of this entity concept is that a corporation cannot derive any rights from its members because it is distinct from them.

What purpose does this entity concept serve? The traditional answer is that it is needed to explain why corporate shareholders possess limited liability. But, as we have seen, limited liability can be explained without inventing an entity. Limited liability for debts is created by an implied contract between shareholders and creditors, while limited liability for torts exists because the rule of vicarious liability does not apply to inactive investors, whether they are limited partners or corporate shareholders.

The entity idea and its corollary—that a corporation cannot derive rights from its members—is false and should be discarded. *Every* organization, regardless of its legal form or features, consists only of individuals. A group or association is only a concept, a mental construct, used to classify different types of relationships between individuals. Whether the concept is a marriage, a partnership, a team, a crowd, a choir, a corps de ballet, or a corporation, one fact remains constant: the concept denotes the relationship between individuals and has no referent apart from it. In a marriage, for example, there are two individuals whose relationship is designated by the concepts of husband and wife, but there is no need to posit or invent an artificial entity to represent the marriage or to account for the fact that in the eyes of the law the husband and wife are regarded as a unit for some purposes (e.g., community property).

If a census-taker were to enumerate three individuals—two real (husband and wife) and one fictitious legal entity (the couple or the marriage)—the error would be obvious. Yet the same error goes unrecognized when the subject is corporations.

The term corporation actually means a group of individuals who engage in a particular type of contractual relationship with each other. Designating their relationship as a corporation is, as Frederick W. Maitland noted in 1900, "a mere labour-saving device, like stenography or the mathematician's symbols."[4] Instead of describing the intricate details of their relationship, which would be tedious and time-consuming, we substitute a shorthand symbol—a concept. But the use of the symbol must never obscure the fact that when rights are imputed to a corporation, what we really are referring to are the individual rights of its members—the shareholders, directors, and officers.

The Separation of Ownership and Control

The primary difference between corporations and partnerships involves agency authority. Because partners are mutual agents, there are, as noted earlier, restrictions on the transferability of partnership interests. But, since shareholders are not mutual agents, there is no need to restrict the transferability of shares. This means that a corporation's capital can be supplied by hundreds, thousands, or potentially even millions of investors, each of whom may be a stranger to all the others.

It also means that a corporation's long-term capital needs can be supplied by a steady succession of short-term investors. Although it is fashionable to disparage short-term investors as speculators whose buying and selling of shares serves no useful or productive function, the exact opposite is true. They provide liquidity for any existing investor who needs or wants to sell his holdings. Free transferability creates instant liquidity; there is no need to obtain the other owners' approval of the proposed new buyer, and there is no time period to wait before one can sell one's shares and no penalty for early withdrawal. Instead, each investor can retain his shares as long as he prefers. It is hard to imagine a more equitable or attractive arrangement.

The corporate form encourages a widening specialization of

function, or division of labor, by enabling some people to invest money which other people will manage. Although this situation is not unique to corporations, critics demand that the federal government compel shareholders to manage their own money personally, as partners do. According to Nader, who totally accepts the thesis of Berle and Means, the increase in the number of corporate shareholders has led to a separation of ownership and control. But that claim is wrong because it *reverses* cause and effect. It was the separation of ownership and control—i.e., the creation of two distinct functions (investment and management)—which made possible the increased number of shareholders. The corporate form flourished precisely because it split the atom of ownership in two. Unlike general partners, corporate shareholders are not mutual agents and do not automatically play an active role in management. And the officers, executives, and managers need not be owner-investors. It is a mutually beneficial relationship for all concerned.

From Partnership to Corporation

At every stage throughout its growth, a corporation is a voluntary association based exclusively on contract. At no stage is it dependent on state-created privileges. One way to demonstrate this fact—the contractual continuum from partnership to corporation—is to trace the growth of a hypothetical firm.

A new business venture usually is conceived by an individual; he has the option of operating it as a sole proprietorship, or if he lacks sufficient capital, he can seek a co-owner, thereby creating a partnership. Then they in turn can add two more partners and then two more again. In less than a decade, a firm which began as a sole proprietorship or a two-man partnership might grow into one with a dozen or more partners. At some point they might find it inconvenient or hazardous to operate with so many individuals possessing agency powers and needing to be consulted on managerial decisions. So they may decide to choose one or a few of them as managing partners and to remove agency powers from all the others. Thus far, their relationship is entirely contractual with no element of state-created privilege.

The original partners had another option. Instead of organizing the business as a partnership, they could have created a limited partnership. They would designate themselves as the general partners, while those who were supplying only capital would become limited partners, a status which gives them no voting rights or voice in management. Because limited partners acquire no agency powers, their ownership interests are freely assignable; that is, they can be sold or given away to anyone.

Like a corporation, a limited partnership is a statutory form of organization, and it must file certain information with a state agency as a way of notifying outsiders. The information to be filed includes the names of the general partners (who bear unlimited liability) and the limited partners (whose liability is limited) as well as the written contract—the articles of limited partnership— which establishes their contractual relationship and sets forth their respective claims to the profits of the firm. Conceptually, limited partnership is the genetic link between a partnership and a corporation, because it establishes a new status—the investor who plays no role in management. (Historically, limited partnership was the transitional stage. Despite the widely held belief that the status of the inactive investor is a perversion introduced by the giant corporations of the twentieth century, this status actually was introduced in the twelfth century by Italian merchants who created limited partnerships, *commenda*, to attract capital from investors who did not desire any role in management or any responsibility for decision making.)

Now imagine that the original group of general partners is growing old; some are eager to retire; others have slowed down mentally or physically. So they decide to relinquish their agency powers and to turn control of the business over to a hired manager to whom they will grant wide discretionary powers. However, to safeguard their investments, they decide to reorganize the firm as a corporation. As shareholders, they can elect themselves directors, which enables them to select the president, closely monitor his performance, and remove him if they so desire.

The owner-directors are well aware that when they die, their heirs may not choose to devote the same amount of time and attention to the business as they did. They realize that some of their heirs may decide to sell their shares to anyone willing to buy them. But they know that they cannot compel their heirs to play an active role in the business, and they know that the business they have built can be carried on by professional managers. They also feel confident that if shares do pass into the hands of strangers, the newcomers will not interfere with the president whom they have selected. Their confidence rests upon the reasonable expectation that those who purchase these shares probably intend to be inactive investors—the corporate equivalent of limited partners—and hence are willing to entrust management of the business to the president whom the owner-directors first selected and later to the person whom the president grooms as his successor.

In two or three decades, a business that began as a sole proprietorship or a two-man partnership has been transformed into a corporation run by hired executives. Most of the shareholders probably are strangers to each other, and each owns only a relatively small amount of stock. They are willing to leave control in the hands of the president, satisfied that if they become displeased with his policies or performance, they can sell their shares. So they seldom, if ever, attend the annual meetings of the corporation. They have not been victimized or defrauded, and they are aware that their initial decision to invest was as uncoerced as their continuing relationship. In short, they recognize that the corporation represents a voluntary contractual relationship between investors and officers for their mutual benefit.

Anyone who claims that corporations have no rights or that they depend upon state-created privileges or that they are not really voluntary or based on contract has an obligation to answer certain questions. At what point in the continuum from partnership to corporations do individuals lose their rights? At what point did the enterprise acquire special privileges, making it a creature of the state? At what point must the enterprise be justified in terms of benefit to society or service to the state rather than the well-being of its owners and officers? And when precisely did the enterprise cease to be an aggregate of individuals who possess rights and become transformed into an entity which has no rights?

Describing corporations as creatures or entities obscures the fact that they actually are associations of human beings. Many years ago Professor Wesley Newcomb Hohfeld observed that

> transacting business under the forms, methods and pro-
> cedures pertaining to so-called corporations is simply another
> mode by which *individuals* or *natural persons* can enjoy their
> property and engage in business. Just as several individuals
> may transact business collectively as partners, so they may as
> members of a corporation—the corporation being nothing
> more than an association of such individuals.[5]

If one keeps this observation in mind, it becomes easier to recognize that anyone who proposes to deny or destroy the rights of a corporation is really attacking individual rights.

Chapter 5

The Ideal of Corporate Democracy

Ralph Nader rejects the idea that a corporation is a private association for the mutual benefit of its owners and officers. On the contrary, he views them as mutual adversaries. In arguing for federal chartering, he portrays himself as the ally and spokesman of the shareholders against the officers. The shareholders need protection, he says, because the officers, aided and abetted by subservient directors, are withholding dividends from the shareholders and are running the corporation for their own personal benefit:

> In nearly every large American business corporation, there exists a management autocracy. One man—variously titled the President, or the Chairman of the Board, or the Chief Executive Officer—or a small coterie of men rule the corporation. Far from being chosen by the directors to run the corporation, this chief executive or executive clique chooses the board of directors and, with the acquiescence of the board, controls the corporation.[1]

Because these autocrats dominate the corporation, its rightful rulers—the shareholders—are impotent and passive, Nader contends.

According to Nader, the shareholders (whom he regards as a homogeneous group) want to be in charge, to play an active role in determining corporate goals and in designing the strategy to achieve those goals. But since the officers do not want anyone to interfere with their autocratic powers, they deliberately withhold the information that shareholders need to make intelligent policy decisions. The officers will not relinquish their autocratic powers voluntarily, and under today's system of state incorporation laws, they cannot be forced to do so. The states, says Nader, have been co-conspirators; they have favored the officers at the expense of the shareholders. Instead of enforcing a code that allows officers to implement only those policies initiated by the shareholders or expressly approved by them, the states have permitted corporate officers to exercise vast discretionary powers.[2]

The only cure for these obvious injustices, Nader says, is federal chartering of corporations. Nothing else can restore the lost ideal—corporate democracy—a system of active control by the shareholders. Before the accuracy of his charges is assessed, it is useful to see what changes he proposes to make in today's giant corporations.

Nader's Blueprint for Corporate Democracy

Nader's goals are to strip corporate officers of their decision-making authority, to make directors completely independent of the officers, and to place shareholders in active control.

He proposes an elaborate new system for selecting directors. At present, directors in large corporations are of two types: insiders and outsiders. The insiders are officers; the outsiders usually are officers and directors of other corporations or individuals drawn from such prestigious organizations as universities, foundations, churches, and banks. This system is to be ended; Nader says that "each federally chartered corporation shall be directed by a purely 'outside' board" and that the officers shall play no role in their selection. Officers are to be forbidden by law to serve as directors or even to vote for directors, no matter how many shares of voting stock, even a majority interest, any officer may own. Nader claims to be opposed on principle to nonvoting shares, but this principle is expendable if those who are disenfranchised are owners who also happen to be officers. He refers to their total disenfranchisement as "the complete preclusion [i.e. exclusion] of operating management from corporate suffrage."[3]

In Nader's plan, all directors would be full-time salaried employees of the corporation. Each director would have a personal, salaried staff of attorneys, economists, labor specialists, and consumer advisers. No director would be allowed to serve simultaneously on two corporate boards; each subsidiary corporation of every giant corporation would be required to have its own board of directors. Interlocking directorates would be strictly forbidden. And by law no director would be allowed to serve more than four two-year terms. Each federally chartered corporation would have nine directors, each of whom would have jurisdiction over a special area: employee welfare; consumer protection; environmental protection and community relations; shareholder rights; compliance with law; profits and financial integrity; purchasing and marketing; management efficiency; and planning and research.[4] Interestingly, the special area of *production* is not considered important enough to merit a director of its own.

Nader proposes that anyone who owns 0.1 percent of a corporation's stock be entitled to nominate candidates for three directorships. The same power would be granted to any shareholder group that consists of 100 or more individuals, even if they each own only a single share. "Six weeks prior to the shareholders' meeting to elect directors, each shareholder should receive a ballot and a written statement on which each candidate for the board sets forth his or her qualifications to hold office and purposes for seeking office. All campaign costs would be borne by the corporation."[5] No other method of campaign financing would be allowed.

Nader believes that shareholders currently are apathetic and uninvolved because they lack access to information. He proposes to end corporate secrecy and promote full disclosure by requiring a corporation to supply every shareholder with the following data: "employment statistics showing the number of women, blacks, and other ethnic minorities working at various employment levels in each domestic plant or office above a minimum size"; the corporation's "investment interest in all other companies, both foreign and domestic"; major contracts with federal agencies, government-financed research and development, and federal grants and loans; the corporate income tax return; the names of the actual beneficial owners of stock now held in trust or in street name; "the annual income of its 30 highest paid executives, their securities ownership, securities options, loan arrangements, and retirement benefits"; and corporate income reported by product, rather than an aggregate amount.[6] He simply assumes, without argument or evidence, that shareholders want and will read and will act on this information.

Nader also proposes a system of shareholder plebiscites, with balloting by mail on all "fundamental transactions"—which he defines as "executive proposals involving the purchase, sale, lease, merger, consolidation, financing, refinancing, dissolution, or liquidation of assets equal to, say, 10 percent of the corporation's total assets or over $100 million, or the authorization of corporate securities in any amount." The board of directors would be required by law to send each shareholder a careful description of each proposed transaction, with an estimate of "foreseeable costs and risks" as well as a summary of the arguments of those who favor and those who oppose the transaction.[7]

But why is corporate democracy the ideal and standard against which Nader compares and condemns the giant corporations of today?

The essence of corporate democracy is that "the shareholders (electorate) choose directors (legislators) who in turn select the managers (executive branch) to administer the enterprise day to day."[8] He offers no argument to bolster this ideal; instead he treats it as self-evidently desirable. But is it? Its most objectionable feature is Nader's attempt to impose a *political metaphor* on a business organization. It is a technique widely used by critics of corporations. They call the articles of incorporation a constitution and then claim that the bylaws are private statutes; they also refer to prices as taxes and to merger agreements as treaties. Invariably they extend the language of politics to business and corporations and then condemn business organizations for not being the political institutions which they were never intended to be. This technique—creating and demolishing a strawman—enables Nader and others to claim that corporations lack legitimacy because there is no organized opposition party to challenge the existing officers.

Nader even insinuates that shareholders are in the same position as citizens in Soviet Russia: "Management so totally dominates the proxy machinery that corporate elections have come to resemble the Soviet Union's euphemistic 'Communist ballot'—that is, a ballot which lists only one slate of candidates."[9] In June 1976, he testified that his proposal for shareholder democracy would lead to "an abolition of the most rigid, totalitarian system that comes under the guise of democratic elections, namely, the corporation's electoral process. The corporate electoral process is an imperfect carbon copy of the way the Kremlin conducts its own elections. In fact, the Kremlin might have learned from the corporations how to develop its processes."[10]

To point out only the most obvious difference in the balloting systems, shareholders are free and able to withdraw their funds instantly from any corporation whose officers or policies they dislike. Nader disparages this choice as being a "love it or leave it" ultimatum. He does not mention that Soviet citizens who do not love it cannot leave it without obtaining permission from their oppressors. Equating the options open to shareholders and Soviet citizens would be comical if it were not so morally obscene.

Corporate Democracy as a Legal Norm

According to Nader, the ideal of corporate democracy is embodied in state incorporation statutes:

> All modern state corporation statutes describe a common image of corporate governance, an image pyramidal in form. At the base of the pyramid are the shareholders or owners of the corporation. . . . The intermediate level is held by the board of directors, who are required by a provision common to nearly every state corporation law 'to manage the business and affairs of the corporation.' . . . Finally, at the apex of the pyramid are the corporate officers. In the eyes of the law, the officers are the employees of the shareholder owners. Their authority is limited to those responsibilities which the directors delegate to them.[11]

He condemns the states for not enforcing adherence to this ideal: "In reality, this legal image is virtually a myth."[12]

He assumes that the pattern described in state incorporation statutes must be eternal and unalterable. Yet his own summary indicates that deviations from the statutory norm are possible; i.e., the authority of officers "is limited to those responsibilities which the directors delegate to them." Nothing in that statement implies a static pattern. When a business is first incorporated, the same small group of individuals are likely to be simultaneously the shareholders, the directors, and the officers. The owners of the most shares almost certainly will elect themselves to serve as the directors, and then acting as directors, they will elect officers from among themselves. Given this close relationship, it is possible— indeed likely—that the corporate president will exercise discretionary authority.

A corporation president can acquire discretionary authority in several ways. One is by an explicit grant from the directors. Another is by making an *unauthorized* exercise of authority—for example, by signing a contract with an outside party, even though the articles of incorporation and bylaws give him no such authority. However, if the directors subsequently approve the unauthorized act, then they have given ratification (the acceptance or adoption of an act done by another person who lacked the authority to perform that act at the time it was performed).[13] Ratification gives retroactive authority. If the newly asserted authority becomes a ratified power of the president, it usually passes automatically to his successors in office. Nothing in this procedure is fraudulent or illegal. The concept of ratified authority is central to the law of agency, which, in turn, is a crucial element of the laws of property and contract.

But there is a third and far more common way in which corporate presidents acquire discretionary authority. The language of bylaws is usually very general and unrestrictive—for example, the president shall be chief executive officer. The exact meaning of that phrase is seldom, if ever, fully specified. Instead, the president usually acts according to his own best judgment of what is beneficial to the business, and depending on the degree of confidence the directors have in him, he may or may not give them frequent or detailed reports on his operating decisions. In companies in which the president is the founder or principal shareholder, the directors are well aware that he is handling certain types of situations without consulting them, and rarely do they either ratify or repudiate his decisions. Situations in which the directors rebuke the president for exercising authority without their approval are so infrequent as to be noteworthy.[14]

There is no uniform rule about presidential authority that prevails throughout the business world; instead, the exercise of discretionary authority varies from industry to industry, and even companies in the same industry do not necessarily abide by the same custom. The exercise of discretionary authority by a president has seldom been challenged by a disgruntled shareholder who sues to undo the consequences; so there are relatively few judicial decisions that delineate the scope of presidential authority. But even if a definitive judicial statement did exist, it would not necessarily be binding upon all companies or industries—unless someone objects and threatens to initiate a law suit against a president who exercised authority far beyond the judicially sanctioned range. This rarely happens.

When a corporation goes public, it is not morally or legally necessary to ask new shareholders to approve the president's past exercises of discretionary authority. The new shareholders have no basis for complaint; they have not been deceived or defrauded. When they purchase shares of stock, their relationship to the corporation involves a contract of adhesion; that is, they buy the shares subject to all preexisting conditions enumerated in the corporate articles and bylaws, including not only all prior delegations or ratifications of authority by the board of directors, but also all implicitly sanctioned exercises of discretionary authority by the president.

Contrary to Nader's claim, state incorporation laws are not *prescriptive* and do not set forth a norm that must be followed; instead, they are *suppletory*. They set forth a norm which applies only if no agreement to modify the norm has been made. (The laws of partnership and of intestacy [dying without a will] serve exactly the same purpose.) As long as no one is coerced or defrauded, *any* pattern should be permissible. But Nader will not tolerate diversity; he wants the law to dictate a universal and unalterable norm. Therefore, he calls for federal intervention.

Federal chartering would prevent a board of directors from delegating its authority; no such delegation would be authorized in the federal charter, and the charter would be unamendable on this point. A board would not be allowed to delegate its authority either to corporate officers or to an executive committee of the board, and the shareholders would not be allowed to authorize such a delegation even if their vote to do so is unanimous. In other words, the shareholders and the directors would be denied the very power which Nader claims he wants to give them—the ultimate power to make decisions.

Corporate Democracy in the Nineteenth Century

Nader believes that because corporate democracy existed in the nineteenth century, it should exist today. He reports that most present-day shareholders do not attend annual meetings; that the proxy votes of absent shareholders are almost always cast in favor of current officeholders; and that today, instead of requiring a unanimous vote, only a simple majority or at most two-thirds is required to approve any fundamental transaction. In contrast, he notes that in the nineteenth century, "the shareholders meeting— much like a New England town meeting—became the critical decision-making forum. At the meeting, any proposal to change the corporation's assets, share structure, capitalization, or by-laws had to be unanimously approved."[15]

Nader laments that many shareholders never bother to vote; he claims this makes a mockery of corporate democracy. Worse still, when shareholders do vote, they are asked to endorse proposals *initiated* by officers. To Nader, this pattern represents an obvious perversion of the democratic process; just as citizens should be the initiators or prime movers in the political sphere, so too should shareholders initiate the policies of the corporation.

Of course, Nader's ideal does not exist today, either in the political or corporate sphere, but he implies that it once did exist in practice—in the late eighteenth and early nineteenth centuries. But, in fact, it did not. He offers no evidence that the political process ever resembled his ideal, and his implied claim is contradicted by a leading historian of colonial America. Referring to voter participation in eighteenth-century America, Professor Edmund S. Morgan wrote:

> Most adult males in the American colonies had the right to vote, but they exercised it only occasionally or not at all. . . . they did not wish to be bothered with it unless they thought the government was up to something worth being bothered

about. Those who cast the majority of votes in an election one year might not take the trouble to vote at all the next year. Sometimes a few of them assembled to give instructions to their representative, but both the gathering and the instructions were likely to have been instigated by the man instructed, who hoped to gain the leverage of popular approval for the adoption of measures that he or his faction already favored.[16]

Nor did the lost golden age of corporate democracy ever actually exist. Nader's only evidence is based on quasi-partnerships, that is, firms whose owners viewed themselves as partners but who nonetheless incorporated their business in order to obtain special privileges from government.[17]

Corporations in the early nineteenth century were *intended* to be partnerships. One contemporary observer wrote:

These institutions were originally organized by a few men, who united their capital like *co-partners*. . . . The *small number of owners*, by devoting their *personal attention*, and by bringing all their shrewdness, energy and perseverance to bear for the welfare of their enterprises, as other *partners* do in the management of their property, were so far successful as to afford a generous employment to industry and a profitable investment to capital.[18]

Their relationship so resembled that of partners that early nineteenth-century courts often applied partnership principles to these corporations. For example, in 1807, a Massachusetts court ruled that a corporate shareholder was entitled to preemptive rights; i.e., he could buy enough shares of any proposed new stock issue to prevent his voting strength from being diminished and his existing percentage claim upon corporate profits from being diluted. The judge's decision stated:

Viewing a corporation of this kind as a *copartnership*, a power of increasing their stock, reserved in their original agreement, is a beneficial interest vested in each *partner*, to which no stranger can be made a party, but by the consent of each subsisting *partner*; and it is a power which the subsisting *partners* must exercise proportionally, and according to their interest in the original stock.[19]

When viewed against this background, Nader's attempt to invoke quasi-partnership as a standard against which to compare today's giant corporations is misleading and irrelevant. *Then*, a corporation had six or twelve shareholders who were intimate acquaintances, viewed themselves as partners, and were prepared to devote "their personal attention" and "all their shrewdness, energy and perseverance" to the business "as other partners do." *Today*, a medium-size corporate giant such as Coca-Cola or Bristol-Myers has 60,000 shareholders, while General Motors has 1,400,000 and American Telephone and Telegraph has nearly 3,000,000.

Rather than being intimate acquaintances, today's shareholders are strangers to each other—residents not merely of the fifty states but often of more than one hundred different nations. If someone today living in Alaska or Arizona, Austria or Australia buys shares in General Motors or U.S. Steel, he hardly views himself as a partner or expects to devote his "personal attention" and all his "shrewdness, energy and perseverance" to that business.

When shares can be easily traded on stock exchanges, it is fairer and less costly to all parties if those who disapprove of policies initiated by a corporation's officers simply sell their shares. Nor is there any need today to protect a shareholder's preemptive rights; he can simply buy enough shares of a new stock issue through a stockbroker to prevent his existing percentage of votes and profits from being reduced. In short, the legal safeguards necessary for shareholders in the early nineteenth century are not relevant today because giant corporations are not intimate partnerships.

Given the low cost of selling one's shares and switching one's funds to another corporation or to some other investment opportunity, it is hardly surprising that dissatisfied investors prefer to sell, instead of expending time and energy to form a coalition of shareholders to oust the existing officers and directors. A policy of 'love it or leave it' makes perfect sense when there are 14,000 publicly traded corporations to choose among. Anyone whose professed goal is to give shareholders the widest possible range of choices would not be able to conceive of or to create the stock exchange system that spontaneously evolved over the past century. Far from being the antithesis of free choice and continuous accountability, as Nader claims, the publicly traded giant corporation is the highest embodiment and expression of these ideals.

Chapter **6**

Why State Incorporation Laws Are Permissive

To make his case for federal chartering, Nader needs to establish that it is constitutional and that state chartering has failed—a case which must be built upon accurate and well-documented scholarship. The issue of reliable scholarship is crucial because Nader intends to inspire a major far-reaching piece of legislation.

Nader and his admirers have repeatedly stressed his accuracy. In 1968, *Playboy* wrote that "Nader has established an untarnished credibility record. 'When I get a story from Ralph,' one reporter says, 'I don't have to double-check his facts.' "[1] In 1972, a sympathetic critic wrote that Nader maintains his public credibility "by satisfying the public that his facts are accurate and well-documented."[2] In 1976 Nader said that to avoid being accused of sloppy work, he and his coauthors "have high standards."[3]

Even those who disagree with Nader's viewpoint and recommendations are impressed by his scholarship. Reviewing Nader's report *Constitutionalizing the Corporation*, a law professor wrote: "The research is extensive and appears accurate."[4] Another professor, reviewing Nader's book *Taming the Giant Corporation*, said: "Its historical materials are well-organized and illuminating, sometimes breaking new ground in popular literature."[5]

Only rarely is Nader's credibility questioned. In 1976, a writer in *The National Observer* charged: "For more than a decade now, many reporters have largely and eagerly suspended their journalistic judgment in reporting on Nader. His pronouncements are taken as truth."[6] Nader replied: "Our studies and actions are reported by the media and accepted by most citizens *precisely and only* because of a tradition of credibility and accuracy."[7]

Nader's response was hardly appropriate. Three months earlier, one of the chapters in *Constitutionalizing the Corporation* had been shown to contain numerous inaccuracies.[8] There were footnotes which failed to correspond to the text, and sources which did not contain the materials he claimed they contained. But, most seriously, he offered bogus documentation for the constitutionality of federal chartering. He wrote: "There is little doubt today that the federal government can charter business corporations." In a footnote, he elaborated: "Although once hotly disputed, there is today no serious question that a federal chartering law would be constitutional."[9]

In support of this opinion, Nader cited two authoritative sources. But the first—a 1969 essay by Adolf A. Berle—makes no mention of the issue of constitutionality. The second reference was to a 1934 Federal Trade Commission report. Now 1934 hardly fits Nader's twice-repeated claim that "today" the constitutionality of federal chartering can hardly be denied. But anyone who managed to track down the FTC report[10] (cited in such a way as to discourage its being found) did not discover an FTC opinion on the page Nader cites, but rather an excerpt from an article by H. L. Wilgus in the *Michigan Law Review*. Since Wilgus (1859–1935) was a reputable scholar, Nader's "authority" does not seem to be controverted, except for one fact: the article was published in February, 1904, not exactly "today."

In response to this disclosure, Nader explained that the footnotes simply were misnumbered and that they would be printed in the correct sequence when the hardcover version was published in September. Mark Green, Nader's coauthor, offered the same explanation: ". . . several footnotes within Chapter III of our offset, preliminary draft were put in the wrong order. Or, as Oscar Wilde once said, 'A poet can survive anything but a misprint.' "[11]

When *Taming the Giant Corporation* was published, it was possible to compare the two versions. The Nader-Green explanation of the errors turned out to be inaccurate and disingenuous. The same chapter (with only a few minor word changes) now contained 28 footnotes, instead of the original 22, but 20 of the 28 were brand-new and had not appeared *in any sequence* in the earlier version. Thus, the false footnotes were replaced, not rearranged. And while every minor point is footnoted, the most important and controversial statement in the chapter is not:

"There is today no serious question that a federal chartering law would be constitutional." In the hardcover edition, this is offered as a naked assertion, with no pretense at documentation or argumentation. The switch from a bogus citation to a dogmatic pronouncement represents a dubious stride toward accuracy.

Of course, it is possible that this incident represents a solitary lapse from Nader's presumed accuracy. Fortunately, we need not speculate because there is an excellent test-case at hand. *Taming the Giant Corporation* contains a chapter entitled "The Collapse of State Corporation Law." It is massively documented, with over one hundred footnotes, a strong indication that it is based on solid scholarship. This was the chapter which one reviewer said broke "new ground in popular literature." In it, Nader attempts to demonstrate that state chartering has failed—that the states destroyed corporate democracy by permitting the officers, not the shareholders, to dominate corporate policy. Are his facts really facts? Does he accurately cite his sources? And do his sources say what he says they do?

Nader's account contains four major elements. First, he claims that James Madison was the original advocate of federal chartering. Second, he believes that the state incorporation statutes passed in the mid-nineteenth century were properly protective of the public interest and of shareholders because these laws restricted corporate activities and limited the authority of corporate officers. Third, he charges that in 1890 a corrupt cabal in New Jersey began the subversion of the state incorporation system by removing the restraints that formerly had been placed upon corporations and their officers. Finally, he alleges that the erosion begun in New Jersey was completed in Delaware, which won the infamous competition between the states for corporate chartering revenues.

Are these charges true?

Nader says that James Madison introduced the idea of federal chartering. At the Constitutional Convention of 1787, Madison urged that the Constitution include a provision authorizing Congress "to grant charters of corporation in cases where the public good may require them and the authority of a single state may be incompetent." What did Madison mean?

Recall that in the late eighteenth and early nineteenth centuries, the primary goal of incorporators was to obtain legally enforced monopolies or other privileges—state loans or subsidies, for example—which otherwise were unobtainable. In other words, corporations were quasi-governmental agencies. When Madison made his proposal for federal chartering of corporations, his aim was to encourage private corporations to construct public works such as harbors and canals using federal funds or subsidies. In 1784–1785, while serving as governor of Virginia, he had witnessed rivalries, which had interfered with internal improvement projects along the James and Potomac rivers, between the legislatures of Maryland and Virginia. Madison wanted such projects to be carried out under federal authority in order to prevent any state from interfering with projects that he believed were essential to the growth of interstate commerce.[12] Hence he favored federal chartering of these quasi-governmental enterprises.

But Nader's proposal bears no resemblance to Madison's. Nader's target—giant private corporations—did not exist in the eighteenth century. Therefore, it is highly misleading to imply, as he repeatedly does, that James Madison was an early ideological ally of his plan.[13]

The General Incorporation Statutes

Nader correctly observes that corporations during the early nineteenth century were unpopular because they exercised "monopoly privileges" and that during the Jacksonian era an important change took place: "The effect of three decades of Jacksonian politics [1828–1858] was to transform the nature of the business corporations. . . . Under the new general incorporation acts, the hated privileges of the special acts were abolished."[14]

But then Nader claims that the general incorporation acts imposed "limitations on corporate size and activity." Is this true? He says: "Every state in the Union limited incorporation to a single purpose or a limited number of purposes, such as a particular transportation, mining or manufacturing project." He also says that the states set limits on the geographic scope of corporate operations, often forbidding them from doing business or owning property out-of-state, and that "the general corporation acts established the power of shareholders to direct the policy of their corporation."[15] He approves of these statutes because he believes they introduced new restraints upon corporate activity.

As a source for these statements, Nader cites *The Modern Corporation and Private Property* by Adolf A. Berle and Gardiner C. Means. When one consults the pages cited by Nader, it turns out that Berle and Means made exactly the opposite point. Whereas Nader says the general incorporation acts introduced restraints, Berle and Means said that the restraints existed only *before* the general incorporation acts were passed, at a time when corporations were still quasi-governmental agencies. They stressed that the limitations previously imposed by the state legislatures began "to recede with the adoption by states of general incorporation laws. These laws resulted in the elimination of the legislature from negotiations attending the formation of the corporate contract. In place of a body [the state legislature] which scrutinized, controlled and might prescribe arrangements, there was substituted a state official, usually the secretary of state, who was obliged to file a document, or charter, which complied with the state laws. The 'contract' was thus drafted by the incorporators."[16]

Berle and Means also reported that the first general incorporation statute was enacted by Connecticut in 1837 and that it permitted incorporation "for any lawful business," which "was not limited to any one business but to as many businesses as the incorporators might name, [so] the rule of a single defined enterprise may be said to disappear."[17] A few western states, e.g., Texas, continued to impose limits on the scope and duration of corporate businesses, but such restrictions were exceptional; nationally, the broad trend toward liberalization prevailed.

Berle and Means, therefore, offer no support for Nader's claims; in fact, their evidence contradicts his conclusions. Although Berle and Means strongly disapproved of the increasingly permissive or enabling character of general incorporation statutes, their integrity as scholars prevented them from inverting or inventing the facts of history.

The Indictment of New Jersey

Nader charges that New Jersey led the way in subverting corporate law. His account is shot through with what scholars call phantom footnotes—that is, citations which prove to be unverifiable and either bogus or deceptive. The errors are essential; without them, Nader has no basis for accusing New Jersey of corruption and dereliction and thus no grounds for attacking the state incorporation system.

In his account of how New Jersey came to liberalize its corporation law in the late nineteenth century, Nader presents a lurid tale of corruption, including the charge that the governor of New Jersey, Leon Abbett, was bribed. As Nader tells it, the story is colorful and dramatic:

> In 1890, James B. Dill, a young New York attorney, took the ferry across the Hudson to persuade the Governor of New Jersey to transform the Garden State into a "Mecca for Corporations."[18]

This sentence contains four major errors. Dill did not take a ferry across the Hudson; he met Abbett, the *former* governor, in Abbett's office in downtown Manhattan, a few blocks away from Dill's own office. Their meeting took place in 1889 (not 1890) when Abbett was out of office; he served as governor between 1884 and 1887 and then again from 1890 to 1893. And, contrary to what Nader implies, Abbett initiated the meeting. Nader's only source for this fanciful tale is a 1905 article in *McClure's* by Lincoln Steffens, a journalist. (He cites other sources but they lend no support to his charges.)[19]

Nader's uncritical dependence on an undocumented article as an authoritative source is noteworthy, as is his preference for a conspiratorial explanation of historical events. He does not disclose that Steffens's article was based on interviews fifteen years after the Dill-Abbett meeting, that Steffens made no attempt to interview Judge Dill, and that Steffens reports that no one whom he interviewed made any mention of Dill.[20]

What, in fact, did Dill do? He made four suggestions, all of which were adopted. In 1888, a year before Dill's first meeting with Abbett, New Jersey had amended its constitution to legalize holding companies.[21] Dill recommended a law which would clarify and elaborate the 1888 amendment. He also suggested a further liberalization of New Jersey's corporation law, which would have continued a trend begun in an act passed in 1875 to permit incorporation for almost any business purpose. And he urged two new safeguards for corporate creditors and shareholders: the first "required a corporation to have an agent in the state upon whom papers could be served, thus excluding the 'tramp' corporation," while the second "prescribed 'private publicity,' or the keeping of adequate records for the protection of shareholders."[22]

Instead of reporting these easily accessible facts, Nader charges that New Jersey adopted Dill's plan "because the Governor, the Secretary of State, and other leading politicians of the state were bribed." Their alleged loot consisted of shares in the Corporation Trust Company of New Jersey, a company Dill formed to publicize the advantages of incorporating in New Jersey and to handle the incorporation formalities for new enterprises. Nader writes: "Abbett was only too happy to accept stock in the Trust Company and serve as a director for the duration of his term in office."[23] His *only* source for this statement is Lincoln Steffens, who explicitly made the *opposite* point—that Abbett paid for his stock and that Abbett's name was not exploited to attract corporations to New Jersey or clients to the Trust Company.[24]

Nader concludes by claiming:

> In 1891 New Jersey went into the chartermongering business. A statute was rushed through the legislature authorizing New Jersey corporations to buy and sell the stock or property of other corporations and to issue their own stock as payment. This "Holding Company" Act effectively legalized the trust organization by authorizing a single corporation to control the stock or assets of its competitors in the same fashion as a trust. Lest anyone misunderstand, in 1892 New Jersey repealed its antitrust law.[25]

Nader's source for these statements is an article by Harold W. Stoke in the October 1930 issue of the *Journal of Political Economy*. But, once again, he has misread or misrepresented his source.

Professor Stoke correctly indicated that the Act which legalized the holding company was passed in 1888 (that is, *before*, not after, Dill's meeting with Abbett, and not in 1891, as Nader claims).[26] And because New Jersey did not enact its first antitrust law until 1913, it could not have been repealed in 1892.[27] As his source for the repeal, Nader cites page 209 of Stoke's article. But there is no such page in that article, and Stoke does not mention such a repeal anywhere in his article. It turns out that Nader gave his readers the page number of another article in a different journal, one which he does not quote or draw upon because, as he explains in a footnote, it provides "a more benign explanation" of New Jersey corporate law than the one presented in Lincoln Steffens's piece.[28] In the "benign" article, by Edward Q. Keasbey in the 1899 *Harvard Law Review*, one learns that, contrary to Nader's claim, New Jersey in 1892 only repealed a minor provision of its criminal conspiracy law.[29]

In fact, Keasbey's article completely contradicts Nader's interpretation of New Jersey's corporation laws and thus deserves to be quoted at length. Keasbey writes that "New Jersey's policy is one of encouraging the aggregation of capital" and that New Jersey

> treats the corporation as an association for the purpose of business, and deals with it as it deals with individuals and partnerships in the conduct of their affairs. It adopts the principle that men, whether associated as partners or in joint-stock companies under the name of corporations, should be allowed all the liberty that is consistent with public safety and order; that freedom of contract is an essential part of the liberty of the citizen, and that the largest practicable freedom of the individual is for the best interest of the community. . . .
>
> The element of stability is an important characteristic of the laws governing corporations in New Jersey. Few changes have been made in the statutes during a long period, and these were made along the lines of development already laid down. The decisions of the courts also have been consistent and uniform. The courts have not been easily disturbed by sudden changes of public opinion with respect to corporations, and the bar has been able to rely upon an orderly devel-

opment of legal principles governing corporate enterprises. Stability in legislation and judicial decision are an important inducement in the choice of a domicile for an organization which is to endure for an indefinite period, and, in view of the possibility of failure and the sudden end of the corporate life, it is also satisfactory for the parents of the enterprise to know that in case of dissolution it will have skillful treatment and decent burial. It is a fact of some importance in determining the location of a company in New Jersey that in case of insolvency, or on dissolution for any cause, the winding up of a corporation is in the hands of a Court of Chancery; and that this is but one court for the whole State, made up of judges set apart for dealing with cases in equity, and acting together with the Chancellor at the head, so that the policy and practice of the court are fixed and well known, and there is no conflict of local jurisdictions with respect to injunctions and the appointment of receivers, and that this court is well known to consist of men of integrity and sound discretion well acquainted with the law.[30]

Keasbey's account does not present New Jersey's corporate statutes as a destruction of democracy or a subversion of justice accomplished by bribery; on the contrary, one sees in his account how a system evolved whose primary feature is *fairness to all participants*. Instead of attempting to refute Keasbey's explanation, Nader simply labels it benign and ignores it.

The Denunciation of Delaware

Nader claims that New Jersey began the subversion of corporate law and that Delaware completed the process. His attack upon New Jersey is mild-mannered compared to his attack on Delaware. He says the states competed to see which one could be the most permissive and irresponsible—the one which imposed the fewest restrictions upon corporations and their officers—and that Delaware won this infamous competition.[31]

Today, Delaware is known as the corporate headquarters of America. In 1974, 448 of the largest 1,000 industrial corporations were incorporated in Delaware, even though most of their major manufacturing facilities and sales outlets were elsewhere. This fact is offered as proof that Delaware prostituted itself by selling its body of corporate law to the highest bidder. Let's test Nader's theory.

What evil does he claim Delaware committed? He quotes a provision from Delaware's 1899 revision of its corporate statutes:

> The certificate of incorporation may also contain any provision which the incorporators may choose to insert for the management of the business and for the conduct of the affairs of the corporation, and any provision creating, defining, limiting, and regulating the powers of the corporation, the directors and stockholders; provided, such provisions are not contrary to the laws of this State.

And he comments:

> These sanguine little words literally turned corporate law inside out. The first hundred years of the corporation's history in the United States had established one rule above all else: The business corporation could only exercise powers explicitly provided or necessarily implied in its charter with the state. Delaware's "self-determination" provision allowed the corporation to be a lawmaker itself. The corporation could conduct business in any way it chose as long as the state did not explicitly prohibit it.[32]

But, in fact, all that Delaware did was to permit flexibility; it recognized that most decisions should be optional, left open to private preference and contractual agreement, rather than being dictated by the state. And if that policy is an evil, it cannot be laid at Delaware's door. In its 1899 statute, Delaware simply copied, almost word for word, an 1898 amendment to New Jersey's corporate law.[33] And, as Keasbey's article made clear, New Jersey already had adopted the same basic policy as early as 1875; and its ultimate root in America was the first general incorporation law passed by Connecticut in 1837.

Berle and Means listed Delaware as the *twelfth* state to enact a permissive or enabling statute: "Connecticut 1837; Virginia 1860; California 1863; Arizona 1866; Maryland 1868; Illinois 1872;

Pennsylvania 1874; New York and New Jersey 1875; Maine 1876; Rhode Island 1893; Delaware 1899; Massachusetts 1902; Alabama 1903."[34] So, far from having turned corporate law inside out as Nader alleges, Delaware actually was a latecomer. It seems fair to conclude that if, as Nader claims, he enjoys the confidence and trust of the public "precisely and only because of a tradition of credibility and accuracy," then he has forfeited that confidence.

The Preeminence of Delaware

Today Delaware is undeniably the leader and pacesetter. Since 1912, 213 of the largest 1,000 industrial corporations have switched from some other state to Delaware, 108 of them since 1967. What explains Delaware's desirability? One factor is low taxes. A business firm can incorporate in any state, not necessarily the one in which its main offices or factories are located; so—all other things being equal—a state can attract firms by charging very low organizational fees for new corporations or those transferring from another state. In addition, a corporation pays an annual franchise tax, based on its capital stock. If the tax rate is substantially lower in one state than another, corporations have an incentive to shift. But a slight savings—or even a substantial one—is seldom decisive.

The biggest factor, one appreciated by Delaware's legislators when they deliberately set out to make their state attractive to corporations, is to provide businesses with the greatest range of flexibility and freedom consistent with the protection of investors and creditors against fraud. In 1913, at the urging of Woodrow Wilson, a reform governor, New Jersey passed legislation that severely restricted corporate activities. Delaware, which previously had been unsuccessful in attracting corporations through low taxes, was the beneficiary of a massive exodus from New Jersey. Although New Jersey's legislation was repealed in 1917, Delaware gained an irreversible advantage; corporate officials saw no reason to switch back to New Jersey's jurisdiction.

In addition to low taxes, the advantages of Delaware today are identical to those described by Keasbey when New Jersey was the leader. The judges for Delaware's Court of Chancery are chosen on the basis of their familiarity with the intricacies of corporate law and finance, which prevents cases from dragging on for years. Increasingly, the appeal and benefit of incorporation in Delaware—to officers and investors alike—has been its well-developed body of judicial decisions on the meaning of virtually every point that might be the subject of litigation. And when there have been ambiguous or seemingly contradictory judicial precedents, the Delaware legislature has eliminated them by periodically revising and codifying its corporate statutes. These features have made it easier to predict court decisions, and thus to avoid litigation which drains the energies and financial resources of all parties. Greater predictability is a benefit to all because it reduces uncertainty and risk.

If, however, it were true that shareholders were worse off whenever a corporation switched to Delaware, then some evidence should be available to substantiate the charge. Nader has offered none. For example, one would expect to discover that sophisticated investors (such as banks, mutual funds, and insurance companies) would shun the shares of Delaware corporations. Or one might present evidence to show that the stocks of these corporations decline in price, at least temporarily, when a switch to Delaware is proposed or consummated. If sophisticated investors felt that the officers were going to acquire a freer hand in making decisions, then these shareholders might sell some or all of their shares. Although the data on stock trading are available to test this hypothesis, Nader has not attempted to prove his charge.

In view of Nader's denunciation of Delaware, one would expect him to advocate the abolition of state charters. Instead, he proposes dual chartering—state and federal.[35] It is an attempt to appease the states; presumably, it would mean that Delaware, New York, Ohio, Pennsylvania and New Jersey, the five major chartering states, would not lose their tax revenues from chartering. But Nader's 1976 proposal for dual chartering directly contradicts what he wrote in 1973 in his book *Corporate Power in America*: "Federal incorporation for national business *supplants rather than complements* state incorporation; . . . *Since state incorporation is the problem, it should not be part of the solution.*"[36]

Nader may hope that the leading chartering states can be so lulled into complacency that they will not mount political pressures or constitutional challenges against federal chartering. But if federal chartering is enacted, giant corporations will have no reason to retain their state charters, and probably there will be no way to compel them to do so. Why pay franchise taxes in exchange for access to state courts when the cases will now be heard in federal courts? Nader doesn't indicate what service or benefit the states will continue to provide to federally chartered corporations.

Federal chartering would create a wholly new set of federal rules and regulations to govern the internal affairs of giant corporations. Because there are no precedents for new rules, the advantage of Delaware and the other leading states—namely, a vast body of judicial decisions—would be wiped out overnight. Hence a switch to federal chartering would be highly inimical to shareholders because it would introduce uncertainties and ambiguities about the meaning of the new law, thus necessitating expensive and protracted litigation to determine exactly what the new federal rules actually mean.

Yet such a costly changeover might be worthwhile if shareholders were being victimized under the existing system of state incorporation laws—by being denied dividends or other rights to which they are contractually entitled—and if they had no recourse. But, as we shall now see, this is not the case.

Chapter 7

Are Shareholders Being Victimized?

Nader maintains that shareholders are inactive because they have been denied access to information about corporate activities. But there is another explanation for their inactivity; it is a deliberate decision for most shareholders. They are attracted to corporate shares precisely because they will not be required to participate in managerial decision making. What they seek is a *sideline* investment, an opportunity to entrust some of their savings to managerial specialists in return for a share of the resulting profits.

Critics frequently denounce the separation of ownership and control in giant corporations; yet it merely represents a widening specialization of function or division of labor. There is no reason why a shareholder must personally manage his own money. If he wants to supply both capital and managerial services, he can become a sole proprietor or a general partner. But why should anyone else protest if he decides to rely on the managerial expertise of others? This is precisely what a person does when he deposits money in a bank, becomes a limited partner, buys shares in a mutual fund, or purchases corporate bonds.

Just as most investors do not seek to exercise managerial authority, so too, when a business goes public, the founding officers and their successors do not intend to relinquish their decision-making powers. For example, when Walt Disney, Edwin Land, and Thomas J. Watson sold stock in their companies to outsiders, they were seeking capital, not advice on how to produce cartoons, cameras, and computers. New investors were never led to believe that they were acquiring managerial powers equivalent to those of general partners. If the relationship between shareholders and corporate officers is mutually acceptable, if millions of people willingly invest in corporations which they will not personally manage, then critics have no right to interfere.

To denounce the largest corporations because shareholders do not directly control their policies or select the officers—to say that they should, that they must because they are the owners—ignores the fact that owners do not exercise any control in some other leading forms of business organization. Limited partners, for example, are owners; yet they have no voice or vote in setting business policy. Similarly, those who purchase certificates in business trusts exercise no control. Like shareholders, trust beneficiaries obtain freely transferable shares with limited liability, but unlike shareholders, they acquire no voting rights. Investment without control is not an evil if the investors freely consent to that arrangement.

In fact, officers and investors are allies, not adversaries. Those who possess savings are able to supply capital to a business enterprise without having to acquire the specialized knowledge needed for managing a business. And the officers, in turn, obtain an opportunity to run businesses whose capital requirements exceed their personal assets. Their contributions to the enterprise are knowledge and ability—knowledge in the specialized fields of production, marketing and finance, and ability in building and sustaining a business, in directing its growth, and in leading its response to unforeseen problems and challenges. Because of their expertise, the officers properly are left free to act without obtaining authorization from the investors. If this inactive role is unacceptable to any investor—whether limited partner or corporate shareholder—he is free to withhold or withdraw his funds.

Nader, however, assumes that shareholders are eager and qualified to participate in policymaking. He does not consider the likelihood that many shareholders are deliberately inactive and uninvolved because it takes too much time to study the information already available to them. A small-scale investor may have more personal and urgent interests to pursue other than studying the financial and statistical data sent by each of the five or fifteen corporations whose shares he happens to own. Time and energy are scarce resources for each individual, and quite rationally, a person concentrates his prime attention on those areas of life where the effects of a poor decision are most intensely experienced. Thus, the more widely diversified a person's investment portfolio, the less incentive he has to closely monitor each situation.

Nonetheless, in the name of shareholder protection, Nader calls for a system of plebiscites by mail on all fundamental transactions. He proposes this expensive and potentially paralyzing new procedure without acknowledging that a less complicated and less costly system already exists. The stock market functions as a daily plebiscite, enabling investors to register their individual reactions without needing to be members of a majority voting coalition.

The primary safeguard for shareholders of giant corporations is their ability to sell their shares instantly. Professor Henry G. Manne has shown that if corporate officers pursue policies which offend or disappoint a substantial number of shareholders, they undermine their own position. A massive exodus or sell-off by disgruntled shareholders depresses the price of the stock and thus makes it attractive for corporate raiders to attempt a take-over.[1] And Professor Burton G. Malkiel has concurred: "A company that has been run by a management group whose major objective is *not* the well-being of the shareholders will become a prime target for a take-over bid. The ever present threat of such a bid is likely to provide a powerful incentive for management to make the maximization of the shareholders' wealth a primary goal of the firm."[2]

But isn't it true, as Nader claims, that giant corporations deliberately withhold dividends from their shareholders? Nader's explanation is that the officers prefer retained earnings: "Corporate executives are frequently owners of substantial blocks of stock and would, for personal reasons, prefer maximum increases in share price, subject to capital gains taxes, to [i.e., instead of] the ordinary tax treatment of dividend income. The interest of many stockholders is exactly the opposite. They average more modest income and would prefer cash in hand now to the possibility of a price increase later."[3] This comparison tries to create the impression that the typical shareholder is relatively poor, perhaps the proverbial widow or orphan from whose mouth the greedy officers and subservient directors seize the dividend crumbs.

Once he has invoked the plight of the shareholders as a means of condemning the officers, Nader has no further sympathy for them. He accuses shareholders of being profiteers, growing ever richer at the expense of consumers. He claims that the largest corporations possess monopolistic or oligopolistic power which they use to overcharge consumers—and the shareholders are the primary beneficiaries: "Oligopoly overcharges shift income from the *average* consumer to the *wealthy* shareholder, contributing to [greater] income inequality."[4] The shareholders undergo an instantaneous transformation; when Nader wants to damn corporate officers for withholding dividends, the shareholders are relatively poor and needy, but when he wants to damn shareholders, they are portrayed as wealthy parasites.

Similarly, Nader switches back and forth on the question whether ownership of corporate shares is becoming increasingly concentrated or increasingly dispersed. Nader's answer is *both*. First, he notes with alarm the increasing *dispersion*: "In the largest corporations, thousands, sometimes hundreds of thousands, of individuals owned shares with the result that in most of these firms no single individual held an important proportion of the total ownership." Later he reports increasing *concentration*; as of 1963, "1.6 percent of the adult population of the United States owned 82.4 percent of all publicly held stock."[5]

But Nader's statistics are invalid. If 1.6 percent owned 82.4 percent of the shares, then how can he also claim that "approximately 50 percent of the stock in the 1,800 companies traded on the New York Stock Exchange is held by mutual funds, life insurance or property and casualty insurance companies, private pension funds (usually administered through commercial bank trust departments), state and local pension funds, foundations, university endowment funds or other institutional investors"?[6] The total exceeds 100 percent. The problem arises because he classifies institutional investors as individual adults in order to be able to condemn the allegedly increasing concentration of share ownership.[7] Because of double-counting, his statements about individual and institutional holdings are meaningless.

Yet it still might be true that the shareholders, whether wealthy or poor, are being denied dividends. If that were true, one might expect to see a steady decline in dividends paid out. What actually does happen? In a study of corporate dividend policy, Professor Keith V. Smith writes: "The board of directors . . . attempts to construct over time an increasing, or at least a non-decreasing, record of cash dividend payments. . . . [and] when it is no longer possible to avoid a dividend cut, directors will make a single cut large enough so that subsequent cuts are avoided."[8]

When Nader implies that shareholders are helpless, that they must be grateful for whatever meager dividends the directors may declare, he overlooks a crucial fact—investors can study the dividend record of different corporations before they decide to buy shares. Among the 1,800 corporations whose shares are traded on the New York Stock Exchange or the 1,100 on the American Stock Exchange, investors can easily discover which companies stress high dividends. This information is readily available in libraries and stock brokerage offices.

Moreover, the alternative to high dividends—retained earnings—is hardly a calamity. Retained earnings increase the value of the stock, and shareholders thereby benefit. Either a company invests its earnings at a profit, which raises the net asset value of each share and thus drives up the stock price, or it keeps the earnings in an idle cash hoard, thus attracting corporate raiders who bid up the price of the stock in their efforts to gain control of the company. Either way, shareholders stand to gain.

Millions of people have a financial stake in the prosperity of America's largest corporations, either directly through purchase of shares or indirectly through pension funds, insurance companies, and other financial intermediaries. Nader claims to be speaking in the name of these millions, but he offers no evidence that they want or need the plebiscites or other reforms which he is demanding on their behalf.

The Assault on Privacy

Nader calls for compulsory disclosure by corporations of any information needed for "official government purposes,"[9] a term he wants to see interpreted as broadly as possible. He rejects the idea that corporations are entitled to privacy (which he condemns as secrecy). He proposes that "no corporation shall be allowed to keep confidential information required by the government unless it can show a substantial and legitimate competitive harm that will occur if the information is published."[10] If read literally, his statement might suggest that he respects bona fide trade secrecy claims. In fact, he wants those claims to be construed as narrowly as possible by federal agencies and courts.[11] His concern for protecting trade secrecy may be doubted in light of his 1971 remark that

> there is no way to determine what a trade secret is. . . . The more I look into the trade secret area, the more I realize that it isn't a trade secret between competitors—they know all about it—it's a trade secret against consumers or against the public.[12]

He also proposes mandatory disclosure of the names of shareholders who own stock in street name or through nominees. "These contrivances," he says, "are only useful to individuals or companies who wish to evade law or public knowledge."[13] He overlooks the fact that everyone has a right to confidentiality, which need not be justified to anyone else. Privacy is not a law-breaking act.

Nader proposes to give the government an unlimited search warrant to comb through corporate records. What is his rationale? He writes:

> In the words of a Supreme Court decision written . . . in 1906, since corporations are creatures of the state, "full and accurate information as to their operations should be made public at responsible levels."[14]

This alleged quotation from the Supreme Court is bogus: *the opinion cited contains no such statement.*[15] The Court did say that every corporation is a creature of the state and a recipient of certain special privileges and franchises. Nonetheless, in this opinion, the Court acknowledged that corporations are entitled to the same constitutional safeguards—substantive and procedural—which apply to individuals, to partnerships, and to all other types of voluntary associations. The Court said:

> We do not wish to be understood as holding that a corporation
> is not entitled to immunity, under the 4th Amendment,
> against unreasonable searches and seizures. A corporation is,
> after all, but an association of individuals under an assumed
> name and with a distinct legal entity. In organizing itself as a
> collective body it waives no constitutional immunities appro-
> priate to such body. Its property cannot be taken without com-
> pensation. It can only be proceeded against by due process of
> law, and is protected, under the 14th Amendment, against
> unlawful discrimination.[16]

On several different occasions Nader has quoted the 'creatures of the state' segment of this opinion, but never once has he
quoted the Court's recognition that a corporation is an association
of individuals who are entitled to constitutional protection of their
rights. Nader rejects this view; in proposing to strip corporations
of any right to privacy and to subject them to unlimited search
warrants, he really is attempting to strip individuals—officers and
shareholders—of their Fourth and Fifth Amendment rights. Yet
no one has protested this assault upon individual rights because
the intended victims are businessmen.

One can imagine the outcry from civil libertarians if a similar
proposal had been made to deny constitutional protection against
unreasonable search and self-incrimination to any other group,
say, to teenagers. Today, teenage boys are undeniably the largest
single group of lawbreakers; yet if Nader had proposed that *all* of
them be kept under special surveillance or be forced to keep
special curfew hours and to carry local and interstate passports
and to register their whereabouts like paroled convicts or be
denied Fourth and Fifth Amendment rights, there would have
been an outcry of protest—and rightly so. The proper principle—
innocent until proven guilty—applies equally to businessmen.

Chapter **8**

Breaking Up Big Business

In his federal chartering plan, Nader proposes to dismantle the giant corporations because they are "monopolistic" and "anti-competitive." He never defines either term, but does indicate that industries are "oligopolistic" whenever four or fewer firms hold 50 percent or more of any market.[1] He charges that giant corporations never compete with each other, either by lowering prices and improving product quality or by making comparisons in their advertisements. Prices only go "up and up"; companies with monopolistic power can charge "a higher-than-competitive price and make it stick since the consumer would lack a cheaper alternative," and they even can raise prices "because consumers may have nowhere else to go."[2]

He also charges that the giants use their wealth to monopolize advertising, instead of engaging in research and development of new products. They prefer safe routine, hence they become bloated, wasteful, and inefficient because they lack the stimulus of brisk rivalry. He endorses Judge Learned Hand's statements that "unchallenged economic power deadens initiative, discourages thrift and depresses energy" and that giant corporations sink into institutional senility because "the spur of constant stress is necessary to counteract an inevitable disposition to let well enough alone."[3] Ambitious challengers are powerless against the financial resources of the giants; if a smaller challenger tries to inform consumers that its product is superior, it will fail because it lacks enough money for a massive national advertising campaign.[4]

Thus the giants of industry are able to stagnate. The result is higher prices for consumers, higher dividends for shareholders, higher salaries and bonuses for officers, and higher unemployment for the employees. Large corporations, according to Nader, find it more profitable to restrict production and raise prices than to increase production and lower prices. Without any attempt at proof, he claims that one-third of America's industrial capacity is idle and unused. And his entire explanation is "because that's the way oligopolies want it." And he adds: "Idle capacity means idle workers."[5] These claims contradict his *only* favorable opinion: "Large business firms, to be sure, have been creators of wealth and jobs, a major reason why our real per capita income has tripled in the past forty years."[6]

Are any of Nader's allegations valid?

When, in his opinion, did the American economy cease to be competitive? He views the pre-Civil War era as a lost golden age of competition: "The hallmark of the Jacksonian economy [1828–1858] was its atomization. Business firms tended to be small, and bought their raw materials and sold their finished goods locally."[7] But this description of competition sounds more like the *absence* of competition; because firms were small and geographically isolated from each other, customers seldom had more than one source of supply for a particular commodity or manufactured product.

In his eagerness to disparage the American economy today, Nader has to invent the good old days. He claims that before the Civil War, competition flourished and consumers enjoyed a rich array of goods at reasonable prices. But this is not historical fact. Consider, for example, the choices open to most Americans— the residents of rural areas and small towns—living in that era. Rather than having access to a variety of shops for products and services, they made most or all of their purchases in small general stores, where the selection was extremely limited. The shop-keepers had little fear that their customers would turn elsewhere because in thinly populated areas there was trade enough for only one seller. Historian Theodore F. Marburgh explains why con-sumers faced very limited choices: "Normally, these rural retail merchants made purchasing trips only once or twice a year, and they stocked, chiefly, staple items that were not subject to style changes."[8] So, in the era when competition allegedly flourished, most consumers faced a monotonously limited selection of products.

Given the limited choice open to consumers in that era, one would expect Nader to approve of the development of the railroad network because it linked all areas of the country.

Instead, he views the railroad network as a calamity which introduced an era of monopolies:

> During the decades after the Civil War, the character of the United States economy was radically transformed. . . . The genesis of a national transportation network and an expanding urban market made possible a new type of business corporation. For the first time, a single manufacturer could dominate not just a local market, not just a regional one, but an entire national market. To the corporation, the advantages of such a national monopoly were obvious. Risk would be eliminated. No longer would rivals compete for markets, or raw materials, or the best locations, or personnel. Without competition, capital would be easier to secure. Money need not be squandered on advertising or independent salesmen or price wars. More importantly, without competition, profits would be assured.[9]

If the growth of the national transportation network helped to spawn nationwide monopolies whose profits were assured without any need for advertising, then why has advertising increased in volume and intensity over the past century? In fact, the development of the railroad system created and strengthened competition; it did not destroy it. The railroads made almost all regions of the country accessible to producers. The sales monopoly of local producers (based on geographical isolation) was broken up by distant producers whose goods were superior in quality or lower in price. Creation of the railroad network left few zones of safety in which local producers could stagnate, immune from challenge by distant competitors. Once again, Nader's history bears no resemblance to the facts.[10]

And his account of competition today is equally inaccurate. He says that giant corporations can build and maintain their market shares by means of huge advertising budgets, but he does not mention that heavily advertised products can fail—for example, Ford's Edsel and DuPont's Corfam.[11] If his claim were true, if a huge advertising budget could make a firm invincible, there would be no way to explain why some of the leading corporations in 1917 no longer exist and why others which survived are miniscule today.[12] And there also would be no way to account for the fact that some of today's largest industrial corporations were created after 1945.[13] Because they obviously were not born as giants (sales over $250 million), it is clear that new and smaller companies can survive and prosper.

Nor is it the case that once a firm attains giant status, it is immune thereafter to competitive challenges by foreign and domestic producers. Zenith and RCA could not ignore the sales inroads of Panasonic and Sony; the market for Gillette and Schick was trimmed by Wilkinson blades; and Kodak had to respond to Polaroid's challenge. Nader offers these very examples as evidence that giant firms fail to innovate, that they spend more on advertising than on research and development.[14] But his examples actually prove the opposite—that giant firms cannot stagnate, that they face continuous competition from domestic and foreign producers, that their huge advertising budgets do not discourage smaller challengers, and that consumers compare new products with those they have been accustomed to using.

In fact, advertising by the giants often helps to create a market for new competitors, who get a free ride on the coattails of the giants. Hertz and Avis, for example, spent millions to popularize the idea of renting a car and thus created a new field which dozens of smaller companies have entered. But high profits not only attract smaller firms; they also tempt other giants to expand into a new field. Xerox, the pioneer of photocopying, faces stiff competition from other major corporations, including IBM and SCM. A huge advertising budget is neither a guarantee against failure nor essential for success. Until a few years ago, Hershey, the giant of the chocolate industry, did not advertise at all; its product was literally a word-of-mouth success. There is no factual basis for claiming that massive advertising by the giants discourages or crushes challengers.

Nader also condemns advertising because it increases the demand for goods and services at the expense of savings and the virtue of thrift.[15] He overlooks a fact obvious to any newspaper reader or television viewer; some of the most persistent advertising is done by banks, savings and loan companies, insurance companies, mutual funds, stock brokerage firms, and other financial intermediaries, all of whom are trying to encourage savings and investment. It is likely that these ads for savings neutralize to some degree the ads for spending and that the net effect of product advertising is to intensify the competition between *products*, not between saving and spending.

Nader's chief complaint against advertising is that it enables giant corporations to sell defective and shoddy products through the use of false, misleading, or uninformative claims. He suggests a remedy: "Before a television, radio or major metropolitan newspaper advertisement could be communicated, each federally chartered corporation would be required to assemble substantiation of each factual claim concerning one of its products."[16] He is not deterred by the fact that prior restraint—a euphemism for censorship—is incompatible with a free society; instead, he worries that it will not work: "There is the danger that increasing penalties for the communication of false information may lead large companies to respond by communicating *no* information. That is, all commercials would become purely 'image' ads." His long-range goal is to make "our primary manufacturing, retail, and transportation markets more competitive. Image advertising is an attribute common to a non-competitive industry."[17] In other words, if the economy were truly competitive, then all advertising would consist of purely factual statements, giving consumers hard bits of information, instead of what Nader calls empty slogans and silly jingles.

It is difficult to evaluate his claim because he does not explain precisely what he means by competition or a truly competitive economy. If he means an economy in which no company holds more than 12 percent of the market in its industry, then his claim that all advertising would be purely informational is still dubious. There are currently hundreds of retail companies in the American oil industry, and none holds a national market share larger than 8.5 percent. Nonetheless, advertising for gasoline is not purely informational. But why should it be? In an economy in which tens of thousands of products and brands are competing, the first thing a seller has to do is to capture the buyer's attention in the form of either clever commercials, striking billboard ads, or attractive packaging. As long as fraud is not perpetrated and as long as consumers are free to try different brands and to compare them, there is no reason to censor the messages from producers to consumers.

From the perspective of businessmen, competition means a process of rivalry for sales and profits. It is naive to believe that the full extent of competition can be gauged simply by counting the number of firms in an industry or by calculating the market share of the four largest firms. Hundreds of companies might be selling very similar products, but unless they are rivals for at least some of the same actual or potential customers, they cannot be called competitors in any meaningful sense. Or only one or two companies may be functioning in a given industry, but that does not prove an absence of commercial rivalry or business competition (unless legally enforced barriers to entry exist, such as the one which protects the U.S. postal monopoly.) The presence of only one or two firms may mean that they have been or are far superior to all of their rivals, that they offer the greatest value to consumers—which was true, for example, of Alcoa before World War II.[18]

The evidence is abundant that giant firms are not immune from competition. Companies within the same industry compete with each other, e.g., Kodak versus Polaroid; companies which produce in very different industries (steel versus plastic, for example) often are fierce rivals in the same sales market; and companies keep expanding into new fields of production, e.g., IBM challenged Xerox in photocopying, and Xerox introduced an electric typewriter to compete with IBM's. In fact, as long as the government does not create legal barriers to entry—licenses, franchises, tariffs, or import quotas—the giants cannot afford not to compete. If they stagnate, they know that eventually they will attract new domestic and foreign rivals or expansion by existing rivals. Nader may believe that giant corporations are completely immune from competitive challenges, but businessmen know that to be a myth. They face the ever-present possibility of financial failure. And if they ever lose sight of that reality, they have some grim, recent reminders—the bankruptcy of the W. T. Grant Company and the Robert Hall Company, for example.

Dismantling the Giant Corporations

Nader claims that giant corporations can stagnate with total impunity, but what is his solution? He proposes that within one year after enactment of the federal chartering law, the Antitrust Division would publish a list of "relevant product markets."[19] This list would be used retroactively to punish corporations whose share of the market exceeds the permissible limits.

Ignoring the unfairness of retroactive legislation, what penalty does Nader propose? If the giant corporations do not "voluntarily" break themselves up into a number of small, completely autonomous enterprises, then the Antitrust Division would seek a divestiture decree from a newly created tribunal: "a specially appointed, five judge Antimonopoly Court." If a corporation loses its appeal, it would be required either "to sell off assets to an existing firm or to establish new 'going concerns'" unless it can demonstrate "that significant economies of scale would make any horizontal divestiture an economically inefficient remedy." If the Antimonopoly Court accepts that argument, it could impose other penalties: "for example, order the defendant to divest itself of vertically integrated suppliers or dealers, order it to transfer technology or patents royalty-free to competitors or forbid the defendant from further expansion in that industry."[20]

In urging the breakup of giant corporations, Nader favors exclusive reliance upon a simple mathematical test of monopoly power. He advocates the use of four-firm "concentration ratios"—calculating the percentage of sales within an industry by the four largest companies. An antitrust action would be initiated automatically whenever "four or fewer corporations account for 50 percent or more of the sales in *any line of commerce* in *any section* of the country in any consecutive two year period within the most recent five years."[21] It is a criterion which leaves no room for discretion—the government must prosecute or else any interested private citizen can sue the government for failing to prosecute.[22]

Nader's enthusiasm for concentration ratios is not diminished by his own admission that they are unreliable indicators. He points out, for example, that they overstate a company's share of the market because the total sales of a multiproduct company are counted in only one category—so General Motors would be counted only under automobile production even though it also makes refrigerators, electrical appliances, and locomotives. He also notes that concentration ratios may understate a company's market share because "they deal with national averages when [i.e., even though] competition usually occurs at the regional or local level."[23] Concentration ratios are also inaccurate indicators because they fail to count substitutes (steel for aluminum, or vice versa) and because they do not include the sales made by foreign producers in the domestic U.S. market.

But concentration ratios are vulnerable to still another objection; they are based on the dubious premise that products and industries or a line of commerce can be defined in some way that is not arbitrary or unrealistic. Are mink and fake fur the same industry? Are real diamonds and synthetic diamonds the same? Are a yacht and a rowboat the same product line? In each case they are, but only if the product is defined in the widest possible usage—furs, jewelry, boats—while ignoring entirely the crucial differences in quality, styling, reputation, exclusivity, and price that make each member of these pairs a distinctly different product or line of commerce. In reality, the competition (i.e., the rivalry for sales and profits) is between mink coats, diamonds, and yachts even though they are products of three different industries.

Anyone who doubts the difficulty of defining an industry should try to classify the following beverages: spring water, coffee, Coca-Cola and champagne. Are they one line of commerce—beverages? Or two—beverages with caffeine and without caffeine? Or are they four—since each one has a unique cluster of attributes? Clearly they are not interchangeable.

In the famous DuPont cellophane case, the Supreme Court had to decide whether moisture-proof cellophane was a unique product with no close substitutes, in which case DuPont would be found guilty of monopolization, or whether certain similar but not identical products were sufficiently similar, in which case DuPont would be acquitted. The government filed its suit in 1947 in the U.S. District Court and lost; so it appealed that verdict to the Supreme Court, but it lost again in 1956. It took nine years to reach the decision that brick, steel, wood, cement, and stone are not competing products because they are "too different," but that cellophane, pliofilm, foil, glassine, polyethylene—while being distinctly different—are sufficiently similar to be considered competing products.[24] Both opinions—majority and minority— were based upon the subjective decisions of the judges, not upon any clear-cut or objective criteria. It was impossible to predict what the Court would decide in that case, or—despite this precedent—what it will decide in a future case of the same sort when nine different justices are asked to decide the fate of a producer.

When a law is so unclear that one cannot be sure what it means or know when one is violating it, it should be repealed or declared unconstitutional ("void for vagueness") but not reinforced with more drastic penalties. Today, nearly ninety years after the passage of the Sherman Act, it still is impossible to know precisely what it means—even though businessmen can be fined and even imprisoned for violating it.[25]

In Nader's judgment, however, the mere fact that a corporation is huge is proof of its criminality—because he regards size per se as an evil. Observe, however, that he holds this belief as an axiom, a self-evident truth. But if one company holds more than 12 percent of the market, or if four companies hold more than 50 percent, whose rights have been violated? Who has been wrongfully deprived of anything? By what right and in whose name does Nader propose to veto the verdict of the marketplace? And why are the rights of producers to be denied in the name of his axiom? If a man described as a consumer advocate proposes to break up companies that have supplied products of proven excellence and acceptability, what would a "consumer enemy" do?

Chapter 9

A Foot in the Door

The 1976 version of Ralph Nader's federal chartering proposal contains a number of revealing changes from the plan he sketched in 1973. In his book *Corporate Power in America* (1973), he recommended federal chartering for the 1,000 largest corporations; he called for the creation of a new federal agency to administer the new law; and he proposed that federally chartered corporations no longer be subject to state incorporation laws. He also hinted that federal chartering was only an interim, second-best solution and that his ultimate goal was some form of international chartering by the United Nations or another world organization.[1] But in *Taming the Giant Corporation* (1976), he reduced the number of companies from 1,000 to 700; he said that no new federal agency would be needed; he called for a system of "dual nation-state chartering"; and he dropped the idea of international chartering.[2]

Although Nader appears to have changed his mind on these features, he has not explained why his new proposals are superior to the old. Nor has he even indicated that he changed his mind. His reasons, therefore, can only be inferred. In switching to dual chartering, he clearly aims to reduce opposition by the states to federal chartering. But what accounts for the other changes?

In 1973 he said: "What is needed is a new agency—call it the Federal Chartering Agency (FCA)—to issue federal charters for major corporations engaged in interstate business."[3] But in 1976 he dropped the idea because it would encroach upon the jurisdiction of existing federal agencies (chiefly the Justice Department's Antitrust Division and the Securities and Exchange Commission). Rather than arouse institutional jealousies, Nader claimed that the new law virtually would be self-enforcing: "The Federal Chartering Act has largely self-regulating provisions with objective standards."[4] Employees and shareholders of giant corporations also "can initiate legal action to enforce the Act. Or a reinforced [i.e., enlarged] SEC and Antitrust Division will enforce clear standards of the law."⁵ The law will be so precise and objective, says coauthor Mark Green, that "I doubt if you would need more than 50 to 100 new staff members at Justice and the SEC combined."⁶

This claim assumes that the criteria will be clear and acceptable to all concerned parties. But consider, for example, the issue of relevant product markets on which antitrust prosecutions would be based. Nader simply assumes that once the Antitrust Division has supplied the original delineations of relevant product markets, no one will challenge them in the courts. Recall the problems of defining relevant product markets for the beverage industry. If one imagines these complexities multiplied across the economy and adds to them the continuous changes in technology, consumer preferences, and price relationships, one wonders how Nader and his associates concluded that a staff of 50 to 100 could enforce this law or that it "has largely self-regulating provisions with objective standards."

The third change—reducing the number of companies to be subject to the new legislation—is the best indicator of the arbitrary nature of Nader's proposal. In 1973, he wrote: "Only the top one thousand interstate corporations—measured by a combination of sales, asset size, market percentage, and number of employees— would be chartered."⁷ Three years later, two of the four criteria were dropped; for some reason, asset size and market percentage were no longer relevant criteria. And the law would apply to only 700 corporations: "The Act [federal chartering] would cover all industrial, retail, and transportation corporations which sold over $250,000,000 in goods or services or employed more than 10,000 persons in the United States in any one of the previous three years."⁸

How did Nader decide upon these particular figures? "By employing a $250,000,000 annual sales figure as its principal criterion, the Act would bypass approximately 15,000,000 smaller business associations yet would reach some 700 industrial, retail, and transportation corporations whose immense size clearly indicates a national impact."[9] But since federal chartering is to apply only to corporations which meet these highly specific criteria, Nader owes the public and Congress some explanation of how he selected them. Why not $300 million in sales or 12,000 employees so that only 500 corporations would be affected, or $200 million and 8,000 so that nearly 1,500 firms would be included? No answer—just arbitrary numbers tossed out as self-evident truths with no mention that only three years earlier he presented different criteria.

In order for the dividing line to be nonarbitrary, Nader would have to establish an objective basis for singling out the 700 largest corporations for restrictions and regulations that do not apply equally to smaller corporations. For example, he could try to prove that the incidence of lawbreaking is greater among the 700 largest than among the next 700. But even if he offered such evidence, and he has not, it still would not justify subjecting the largest 700 to special restrictions. There can be no justification for a verdict of collective guilt. Each corporation should be judged on its own conduct; size alone does not make a corporation a criminal or a member of a criminal class.

In fact, whether federal chartering applies to 700 or to 1,000 companies is only an insignificant detail, one on which Nader can obligingly give ground or offer to compromise. His goal is to win acceptance of the *principle* of federal chartering. Once he has successfully thrust a foot in the door—once Congress has accepted *any* version of federal chartering—Nader will have won. The whole issue will then become one of quibbling over details, and no one will be able to argue effectively against extending federal chartering to the next hundred or the next thousand largest companies. This foot-in-the-door strategy was confirmed by Nader's coauthor, Joel Seligman. When asked why Nader's proposal is limited to only 700 companies despite the fact that other advocates of federal chartering want it to apply to at least several thousand companies, Seligman answered: "It's unrealistic to try to persuade Congress to pass a bill of this significance for thousands of corporations."[10] Thus, Seligman admitted that political expediency had become the primary consideration for "the forces of goodness," the term he uses to describe those who support Nader.[11]

International Chartering

The fourth change made in 1976 was to delete international chartering as the ultimate goal. In 1973, Nader wrote: "To control national or multinational power requires, *at the least,* national authority."[12] The phrase "at the least" suggests that *federal* chartering is only a short-term solution. But there is more than logical inference to support this conclusion. In September 1973, Nader addressed a special United Nations panel known as "The Group of Eminent Persons" to alert them to the alleged menace of multinational corporations:

> The trouble with multinational corporations, in a word, is accountability. Business is worldwide; government or law is not. Consequently, worldcorps [i.e., multinational corporations] are free of effective control. And lacking accountability, they lack legitimacy . . . To whom are they responsible? To those who govern them [i.e., to corporate officers and directors]. Who are they? A self-perpetuating oligarchy.[13]

To whom did Nader address his attack on corporate oligarchy and his plea for international corporate democracy? To the representatives of Leonid Brezhnev of the U.S.S.R., of Mao Tse-tung of the People's Republic of China, of Fidel Castro of Cuba, of Idi Amin Dada of Uganda, of Indira Gandhi of India, of Juan Peron of Argentina, and other world leaders whose everlasting devotion to democratic principles and institutions was beyond doubt. He urged these paragons of legitimacy and accountability to take immediate action to prevent oligarchies like Xerox, IBM, Coca-Cola, Holiday Inns, Kentucky Fried Chicken, and Walt Disney Enterprises from extending their despotic tyranny over the world.

Nader warned his audience that they must act quickly: "The time is late but the opportunity remains to finally hold these firms accountable to more than their profit statements." As an alternative to corporate oligarchy, he proposed a form of international chartering:

A basic way to hold corporations, even international corporations, more structurally accountable, is to build controls into their birthright—the corporate charter. . . . The problem, however, is that many nations [e.g., Switzerland, Liechtenstein, and Monaco] have weak chartering laws in order to induce corporations to remain or locate there. Thus all are driven down to the lowest common denominator in the competition for corporate business. As a preliminary step, nations could be encouraged, under U.N. initiatives, to formulate parallel and strict terms in their chartering mechanism, covering such areas as corporate disclosure, antitrust, shareholder rights, management liabilities, and affirmative duty to report on a wide variety of matters to all nations where the firm is doing business.[14]

How would international chartering standards be set, and what would be the likely results? If the vote on chartering provisions is based on population, then the terms will be dictated by China and India and a few other extremely poor but heavily populated nations. On the other hand, if voting is based on one vote per nation, then a coalition of Arab, African, and Latin American nations will dominate the vote. Either way, one can imagine the prospects for American corporations should they be forced to stand trial before an International Antimonopoly Court.

In 1976, Nader temporarily dropped the idea of international chartering, until the principle of federal chartering wins congressional acceptance.

Closing All Exits

If federal chartering is adopted, what alternatives will be open to corporations? Nader anticipates that they might try to escape by reincorporating overseas. His remedy is to extend the law to cover all *foreign* corporations whose sales in America exceed $250 million.[15] He also realizes that giant corporations might decide to split themselves into two or more independent companies in order to bring their sales and employment figures below the limits of the law's coverage. He has blocked that exit also. His solution is to decree that "once an active corporation is incorporated under the Federal Corporate Chartering Act, it must remain so."[16]

Although Nader has excluded business trusts from his federal chartering proposal, trusts do possess such corporate attributes as perpetual duration, limited liability, and freely transferable shares. Because corporations might try to reorganize as trusts to avoid the new legislation, Nader has sealed off this escape route too, by making the federal chartering law retroactive for three years.[17] And, in 1976, he also widened the scope of federal chartering. The preliminary version of his proposal, published in January 1976, said that the Act would cover corporations that exceeded $250 million in sales or employed more than 10,000 persons in the U.S. but *only* if these corporations "were listed on a national securities exchange or held of record at least 2,000 American shareholders."[18] In other words, large *privately held* corporations were to be excluded. Eight months later, Nader deleted the stock exchange listing as a precondition of federal chartering; henceforth the law "would apply to such privately held behemoths as Deering Milliken, Hallmark Cards, Hearst Publications, and Cargill."[19]

In view of this sweeping expansion of coverage, it seems puzzling at first that Nader continues to exclude certain types of businesses, regardless of their size: "Banks, insurance companies, public utilities, not-for-profit corporations, cooperatives, and all unincorporated associations would be specifically excluded from the Act."[20] He does not explain why he excludes them, even though it is obvious that he really opposes all large-scale businesses, not merely giant corporations. If he is willing to admit that size per se is his target, then he should explain why he excluded all noncorporate businesses, regardless of size. However, if he says he is only opposed to giant-sized corporations, he would have to claim that only a corporation can be giant-sized. But that is blatantly untrue; corporations are not the only giant enterprises. A few decades ago, Baldwin Locomotive and Gimbel Brothers were giants by the standards of that era; yet they were operated as partnerships. Several decades earlier, at the turn of the century, one of the three largest firms in America, the Carnegie Steel Company, was organized as a limited partnership. And today, at least one of the giant enterprises listed on the New York Stock Exchange is a business trust—the Mesabi Trust. So are the multi-billion dollar REITs (real estate investment trusts) and many of the mutual funds, such as the Massachusetts Investors Trust, which has more than 200,000 investors and over $2 billion in assets.[21] Clearly, giant size does not require incorporation, and equally clearly, incorporation is not a prerequisite for attaining giant size.

There are three other possible explanations for why Nader excludes noncorporate businesses, regardless of size. Perhaps he finds corporations are the only objectionable form of business organization because they are not directly managed by their owners—but this is false; the exact same situation exists in limited partnerships, business trusts, and cooperatives. Or perhaps he thinks that only corporations possess such corporate features as limited liability—but this too is false; these are all optional features of partnerships, limited partnerships, and business trusts. Another possibility is that he believes that the corporate form permits or encourages faster growth and larger size than is possible with any other form of business organization—but that too is false, witness the explosive growth of mutual funds and REITs.

The only remaining possibility is that his exclusion of non-corporate businesses is a strategic ploy—that he temporarily confines his proposal to business corporations because he can cash in on widespread confusion about their nature and legitimacy.

Nader also does not explain why he excludes nonprofit corporations, such as colleges and universities, churches and charities, foundations and professional societies. By incorporating, they all obtain the same features as those shared by business corporations; they acquire entity status, perpetual existence, and limited liability. If one follows Nader's premise to its logical conclusion, the nonprofit corporation is fully as much a creature of the state as any business corporation.

Moreover, if his concern is with organizations "whose immense size clearly indicates a national impact," then the impact on American society of nonprofit corporations often equals and sometimes surpasses those of giant businesses. The Catholic

Church, for example, owns assets in America of $10 billion, has an annual income of $600 million, and employs 167,000 people.[22] It also violates all the criteria Nader uses to justify federal chartering. It does not practice corporate democracy—its members (laity and clergy) cast no votes for its board of directors, the College of Cardinals, or for the pope. Instead, the pope selects the cardinals who, in turn, select the next pope. Neither does the Catholic Church hold plebiscites by mail on all fundamental transactions, nor does it disclose its finances or the number of women, blacks, and other ethnic minorities holding positions at every rank. Most other religious groups—the Mormons, Christian Scientists and Jehovah's Witnesses, for example—also fail to conform to Nader's preferences. Should they, then, be subject to federal chartering? Nearly everyone would answer no, because the First Amendment forbids governmental interference with the free exercise of religion.

But to Nader the First Amendment is expendable. Even though it clearly states: "Congress shall make no law . . . abridging the freedom of speech, or of the press," Nader has proposed federal chartering of America's largest newspapers, magazines, television networks, newspaper chains, and book publishers. The 700 largest corporations include the publishers of the *Washington Post, New York Times, Newsweek, Time,* the *Wall Street Journal,* and *Barron's,* as well as CBS, ABC, and RCA (the corporate parent of NBC), and such leading publishers as Macmillan and McGraw-Hill.[23] Because these corporations disseminate ideas and information, their right to function freely should be inviolable under the First Amendment. Instead, because they are business corporations, Nader proposes to subject them to legislation that would give future administrations a well-stocked arsenal of weapons to intimidate or retaliate against critics. For example, the Antitrust Division could recalculate and redefine the relevant product markets in which these firms operate and then announce that they must be broken up because their market shares exceed the permissible limit. The obvious candidates for this harassment would be the networks, the *New York Times* and the *Washington Post, Time* and *Newsweek.* If Nader can suggest giving the federal government a weapon to stifle criticism and curtail the freedoms of speech and of the press, then there is no reason to believe he is any more dedicated to protecting the freedom of religion guaranteed by the First Amendment.

Nader also recommends that the federal government demand verification of advertising claims made on behalf of commercial products: "The Act would require that major advertisements by federally chartered firms be substantiated."[24] But if the government is to attest to the accuracy of advertising for deodorants, dry cereals, or detergents, then on what basis can it be denied authority to certify the truthfulness of college lectures, church sermons, newspaper editorials, and television news broadcasts? Surely these messages are at least as important as advertising jingles and billboard slogans.

In truth, Nader's blueprint for federal chartering of business corporations is only the first step, not the final destination. He currently limits his plan to business corporations because he can cash in on centuries of confusion about their nature and origins. But once their subjugation is accomplished, the forces of goodness can nominate other candidates for federal chartering.

Of course, Nader does not disclose that his eventual target is *all* large businesses, not merely corporations, and *all* large corporations, not merely businesses. But what other conclusion can one reach after seeing him repeatedly call giant corporations "private governments"?[25] Instead of providing a precise definition, he quotes someone else's murky observation that "they have a direct and decisive impact on the social, economic and political life of the nation."[26] That criterion fits business and nonprofit corporations equally well; it applies not only to General Motors but also to Harvard University, the Brookings Institution, the Ford Foundation, the AFL-CIO, and the major religious denominations. Indeed, as the Supreme Court has observed, there is no inviolable border between freedom of commerce and freedom of ideas. If one is threatened, so is the other.

The effect of calling large businesses "private governments" is to obliterate the distinction between politics and economics, between governments, which can compel obedience to their laws, and businesses, which can succeed only by offering something of value in uncoerced exchange. A business, no matter how large, cannot force anyone to work for it, to buy its products, or to invest in it; it cannot conscript capital and manpower or tax a person to pay for a service he neither wants nor uses. One has to try very hard not to notice the difference.

The power of giant corporations serves as Nader's pretext for federal chartering. But power—a concept he frequently invokes but never defines—is not inherently sinister. The general meaning of power is the ability to achieve some desired goal or result. But, as Ayn Rand identified, political power and economic power are two distinct types.

> No individual or private group or private organization has the legal power to initiate the use of physical force against other individuals or groups and to compel them to act against their own voluntary choice. Only a government holds that power. The nature of governmental action is: *coercive* action.
> . . . What is economic power? It is the power to produce and to trade what one has produced. In a free economy, where no man or group can use physical coercion against anyone, economic power can be achieved only by *voluntary* means: by the voluntary choice and agreement of all those who participate in the process of production and trade. . . . Economic power is exercised by means of a *positive*, by offering men a reward, an incentive, a payment, a value; political power is exercised by means of a *negative*, by the threat of punishment, injury, imprisonment, destruction.[27]

The goals of corporations are increased sales and profits, and to achieve these goals they marshal wealth and resources to be able to offer customers something of value. Economic power is the only power that corporations, large or small, should be able to wield in a capitalist system.

But many people fear something quite different today about the power of giant corporations, and their apprehension is well-justified. In today's mixed economy, corporations often are aided by political power; that is, they are the beneficiaries of various legal restrictions placed upon free trade. Many companies are shielded from both domestic and foreign competition by means of subsidies, loan guarantees, protective tariffs, import quotas, and arbitrary licensing requirements. These restrictions can be created and sustained only by political power—by invoking the threat of governmental intervention to forbid or penalize various forms of production and trade. People rightly fear that corporations, alone or in clusters, can exercise political power and manipulate the government in order to obtain special favors and privileges at the expense both of other companies and of consumers. Corporate power is to be feared only when it involves attempts to secure favors and achieve results that could never be obtained in a free market.

There is no justification for allowing any private individual or business organization, including corporations of any size, to achieve its goals by means of political power. A century ago, a leading commentator on the American scene, E. L. Godkin, warned that chicanery and corruption are inevitable and cannot be eradicated as long as government has favors to bestow. Godkin offered a solution: stripping Congress of the power to confer valuable privileges upon anyone, including business corporations. But this solution does not appeal to Nader. He prefers to institutionalize the idea that if any private business grows beyond some arbitrarily defined size or some undifferentiated degree of power, then government should dictate its internal structure and decision-making mechanism.

Nader's Utopia

Federal chartering is only the first step on a long journey. We are entitled to know the final destination: Nader's vision of an ideal society. But it is a subject he rarely discusses. He told an interviewer that he has never written a philosophical manifesto because "no one reads the great books any more."[28] So his philosophy must be pieced together from the hints scattered in his numerous articles, interviews, and reports.

Nader's critics usually call him a statist because he attacks business and calls for greater governmental controls. But for Nader, statism is only a transitional stage. Once the government has extinguished all existing large-scale private organizations, a new phase of mankind's history can be inaugurated.

What is his ideal society? Nader wants people to live in small, self-sufficient communities where "they can grow their own gardens, they can listen to the birds, they can feel the wind across their cheek [sic], they can watch the sun come up. And within a five-or-six block perimeter, they find they have their stores, their schools. They have their parks, they have their libraries . . . compared to a big city where all of these things are miles away."[29]

In order to make this vision a reality, giant corporations have to be broken up and their individual plants and factories transformed into cooperatives owned by their customers, not by their workers who might, Nader fears, pursue their own advantage rather than making service to the community their highest ideal. Similarly, banks and insurance companies would be transformed into locally controlled, consumer-owned cooperatives run on the basis of one vote per person. This system would constitute the nucleus of what Nader calls "a consumer-owned economy."[30]

Nader opposes reliance upon specialists or organizations; instead, he favors participation by everyone—probably mandatory.[31] If most people preferred to pursue their private interests instead of turning out for public meetings and debates, the system would disintegrate into rule by an activist elite, the ones with the most evenings to spare, the ones willing to put aside all private interests. Therefore, to help make *everyone* a community activist, Nader calls for "a radical transformation of time use. That's the most important single thing. As long as people think that their time is to be divided up into three categories—work, family, and leisure—nothing is going to change. There's got to be a fourth category: the amount of time people spend on their civic obligations."[32]

In a 1971 interview, Nader voiced his belief that individuals must be prepared to sacrifice their leisure and personal goals in order to serve society. "The basic point . . . is to develop what in ancient Athens was called the public citizen, with the main difference being that we don't have slaves like ancient Athens, which made it easy for public citizens. *But we have an affluent society and a lot of spare time.*"[33] This statement reflects his premise that wealth belongs to society as a whole, not to individuals, and that spare time is a free-floating social asset.

As an admiring former associate wrote: "Nader's citizen is strikingly similar to the citizen glorified by Rousseau whose supreme desire was to 'fly to the public assembly.' Nader's citizenship, like Rousseau's, would leave little time for anything else; 'so much the better,' both would say. Sacrifice for the common good is the essence of such citizenship."[34]

Rousseau's *The Social Contract* (1762) seems to be the seminal source of Nader's political philosophy. According to Rousseau, "the better constituted a State is, the more do public affairs occupy men's minds to the exclusion of their private concerns." "In Rousseau's utopia," writes Professor J. L. Talmon, "human egotism must be rooted out, and human nature changed. . . . The aim is to train men to 'bear with docility the yoke of public happiness,' in fact to create a new type of man, a purely political creature, without any particular private or social loyalties, any partial interests, as Rousseau would call them."[35] To achieve this goal, Rousseau stresses that men must live in small communities which enforce "great simplicity of manners" and "a large measure of equality in rank and fortune."

For Rousseau and his intellectual descendants, the appeal of a small community is that it will be easier to enforce self-renunciation and conformity. Proximity and visibility mean that everyone can monitor everyone else's attitudes and actions; there is no chance for escape from constant surveillance. It is a paradise for inquisitors and informers, but a living hell for those who value privacy, independence, and personal freedom.

If Nader found the basic blueprint of utopia in Rousseau's writings, he found the details of implementation in a 1971 essay by Gar Alperovitz.[36] Nader has never quoted Alperovitz's writings, but in 1976 a few months after Alperovitz called for the total destruction of giant corporations, Nader recommended him to President-elect Carter for an appointment to the Council of Economic Advisers—as a man with fresh ideas and insights to contribute to the nation.[37]

Like Nader, Alperovitz favors dismantling the giant corporations and opposes turning their plants and factories over to the workers. Instead:

workers' control should be conceived in the broader context
of, and subordinate to, the entire community. In order to
break down divisions which pose one group against another
and to achieve equity, accordingly, the social unit at the heart
of any proposed new system should, so far as possible, be
inclusive of all the people—minorities, the elderly, women,
youth."[38]

Alperovitz holds that "the only social unit inclusive of *all* the
people is one based on geographic contiguity." In "small, terri-
torially-defined communities," there will be no conflicts of interest
between individuals or groups and the community as a whole;
everyone will be both a resource of the community and a
beneficiary. Instead of individuals choosing their own careers,
"the entire community . . . may decide how to divide work equi-
tably among all its citizens." In such a system, "Individuals are
neither paid nor valued according to their 'product,' but simply
because of their membership in the community."[39]

The eventual goal of the new system will be "universal equality."[40] As a means to that end, Alperovitz suggests:

progressively narrowing the range of inequality by setting
(and gradually lowering) maximum income ceilings, by setting
(and gradually raising) minimum income floors, and by regu-
larly introducing a greater share of such *free goods* as educa-
tion, medical care, housing, and basic food stuffs. Over a
specified period—say, 25 years—it might be possible to
achieve complete equality, perhaps through raising minimum
income levels by 3 percent per annum—and progressively
lowering the ceiling on incomes through taxation and other
means by another 1 percent per annum.[41]

The key to making the whole system work will be to reduce
"individual and community motivation for exorbitant living
standards"[42]—presumably a willingness to forego any comforts or
conveniences produced by one's own labor as long as anyone,
anywhere, for any reason, has less. This system promises to
deliver us from the present-day tyranny of giant corporations,

which want to inflict on us sports cars, stereo sets, calculators and cameras, and other forms of material enslavement.

The world has come full circle in a century; capitalism was denounced a hundred years ago because the workers allegedly were sinking deeper and deeper into misery. Socialist theorists proclaimed the Iron Law of Wages: workers would never earn more than the barest amount required to keep alive and breed children for the work force of the next generation. Today, in contrast, we are told that the evil of capitalism is prosperity and that giant corporations must be destroyed because they depend on and are committed to economic growth, rather than retrenchment. The major industrial corporations are the primary producers and transmission belts of American prosperity; they encourage and cater to individuals who have personal interests and who seek wealth, comfort, and pleasure. That is why they have to be destroyed.

A proper defense of corporations must stress that they are created and sustained by freedom of association and contract, that the source of freedom is not governmental permission but individual rights, and that these rights are not suddenly forfeited when a business grows beyond some arbitrarily defined size, either in terms of assets, sales, and profits or the number of investors, employees, and customers.

The owners and officers of corporations constitute a minority of citizens in America today, but no other minority (economic, racial, religious, or intellectual) is continually forced to justify its right to exist in terms of service to society or the state. Because corporations are *not* autonomous entities, which somehow exist apart from the individuals who own and operate them, any encroachment upon the rights of these individuals establishes a precedent for inroads upon the rights of other individuals, other minorities, and other voluntary associations. That is why *everyone*—not merely business executives and investors—has a crucial stake in defending the corporation.

Notes

Prologue

1. Irving Kristol, "On Corporate Capitalism in America," *Public Interest* 41 (Fall 1975):125, 137.

2. John Kenneth Galbraith, "What Comes After General Motors," *New Republic*, Nov. 2, 1974, p. 16.

3. Adolf A. Berle, Jr. and Gardiner C. Means, *The Modern Corporation and Private Property* (New York: Macmillan, 1932), pp. 345–351.

4. *New York Times*, Oct. 31, 1971, p. 63; Robert A. Dahl, "Governing the Giant Corporation," in *Corporate Power in America*, ed. Ralph Nader and Mark J. Green (New York: Grossman Publishers, 1973), p. 11.

5. See Eileen Shanahan, "Reformer: Urging Business Change," *New York Times*, Jan. 24, 1971, sec. 3, p. 9; Ralph Nader, "The Case for Federal Chartering," in *Corporate Power in America*, pp. 67–93; Ralph Nader, Mark Green, and Joel Seligman, *Constitutionalizing the Corporation: The Case for the Federal Chartering of Giant Corporations* (Washington, D.C.: Corporate Accountability Research Group, 1976); Ralph Nader, Mark Green, and Joel Seligman, *Taming the Giant Corporation* (New York: W. W. Norton & Co., 1976).

Chapter 1

1. Frederick W. Maitland, "Introduction," in Otto von Gierke, *Political Theories of the Middle Ages* (Cambridge: Cambridge University Press, 1900), p. xxx.

2. Joseph K. Angell and Samuel Ames, *A Treatise on the Law of Private Corporations Aggregate* (1832; reprint ed., New York: Arno Press, 1972), pp. 37–50.

3. See A. L. Poole, *Obligations of Society in the XII and XIII Centuries* (Oxford: Clarendon Press, 1946), pp. 76–94; the quote appears on p. 92.

4. Robert L. Raymond, "The Genesis of the Corporation," *Harvard Law Review* 19 (1906):356; on tax farming, see M. M. Postan, E. E. Rich, and Edward Miller, eds., *The Cambridge Economic History of Europe* (Cambridge: Cambridge University Press, 1965), 3:437—438.

5. William S. Holdsworth, *A History of English Law*, 3rd ed. (London: Methuen & Co., n.d.), 3:479, quoting Blackstone's *Commentaries* I, 457.

6. Cecil Thomas Carr, "Early Forms of Corporateness," in *Select Essays in Anglo-American Legal History*, ed. Association of American Law Schools (Boston: Little, Brown & Co., 1909), 3:177—181.

7. Charles Gross, *The Gild Merchant: A Contribution to British Municipal History* (1890; reprint ed., Oxford: Clarendon Press, 1964), 1:43.

8. Samuel Williston, "The History of the Law of Business Corporations Before 1800," in *Select Essays in Anglo-American Legal History*, ed. Association of American Law Schools, 3:198—199.

9. Edmund Bayly Seymour, Jr., "The Historical Development of the Common-Law Conception of a Corporation," *American Law Register* 42 (1903):537—538.

10. Holdsworth, op. cit., 3:471—472.

11. Frederick W. Maitland, "Trust and Corporation," in *Selected Essays*, ed. H. D. Hazeltine, G. Lapsley, and P. H. Winfield (1936; reprint ed., Freeport, N.Y.: Books for Libraries, 1968), pp. 157—158.

12. Austin W. Scott, "Charitable Trusts," in *Encyclopedia of the Social Sciences*, ed. E. R. A. Seligman (New York: Macmillan, 1932) 3:338—340.

13. "The Case of Suttons Hospitall," 10 Coke Rep. 1a, 32b, 77 Eng. Rep. 937, 973 (K.B., 1613).

14. Dartmouth College v. Woodward, 4 Wheat. 518, 636, 4 L. Ed. 629, 659 (1819).

15. Julius W. Goebel, Jr., *Cases and Materials on the Development of Legal Institutions* (Brattleboro, Vt.: Vermont Publishing Co., 1946), p. 389.

Chapter 2

1. Ralph Nader, Mark Green, and Joel Seligman, *Taming the Giant Corporation* (New York: W. W. Norton, 1976), pp. 15, 33—35, 63.

2. Adolf A. Berle, Jr., "The Theory of Enterprise Entity," *Columbia Law Review* 47 (1947):343; Robert W. Hamilton, "The Corporate Entity," *Texas Law Review* 49 (1971):979.

3. Adolf A. Berle, Jr. and Gardiner C. Means, *The Modern Corporation and Private Property*, rev. ed. (New York: Harcourt, Brace & World, 1968), p. 120, n. 2.

4. Alan R. Bromberg, *Crane and Bromberg on Partnership* (St. Paul: West Publishing Co., 1968), pp. 476—477, 509—516.

5. Berle and Means, op. cit., p. 120, n. 2.

6. See Chester Rohrlich, *Organizing Corporate and Other Business Enterprises*, 4th ed. (New York: Matthew Bender, 1967), p. 213; Bromberg, op. cit., pp. 29, 127.

7. See Bromberg, op. cit., p. 19, n. 36, 342, 347–351.

8. Frederick G. Kempin, Jr. and Jeremy L. Wiesen, *Legal Aspects of the Management Process*, 2nd ed. (St. Paul: West Publishing Co., 1976), pp. 168–169, 172, 450–451; William L. Prosser, *Handbook of the Law of Torts*, 4th ed. (St. Paul: West Publishing Co., 1971), pp. 458–459.

9. Dartmouth College v. Woodward, 4 Wheat. 518, 636, 4 L. Ed. 629, 659 (1819).

10. Nader et al., *Taming the Giant Corporation*, p. 138.

11. Stuart Bruchey, "Corporation: Historical Development," in *The Changing Economic Order: Readings in American Business and Economic History*, ed. Alfred D. Chandler, Stuart Bruchey, and Louis Galambos (New York: Harcourt, Brace & World, 1968), p. 140.

12. William Meade Fletcher, *Cyclopedia of the Law of Private Corporations* (Mundelein, Ill.: Callaghan & Co., 1963), 1:21.

Chapter 3

1. Ralph Nader and Mark J. Green, "The Case for Federal Charters," *Nation*, Feb. 5, 1973, p. 173. Four different variations on his concept of the charter can be found in Ralph Nader, "Chartering Corporations," *New Republic*, March 11, 1972, p. 9; Ralph Nader, "The Case for Federal Chartering," in *Corporate Power in America*, ed. Ralph Nader and Mark Green (New York: Grossman Publishers, 1973), p. 80; Ralph Nader and Mark Green, "Is the 'Worldcorp' Above the Law? Time for the U.N. to Move," *War/Peace Report*, Sept./Oct., 1973, p. 7; and Testimony of Ralph Nader, June 17, 1976, in U.S., Congress, Senate, Committee on Commerce, *Hearings: Corporate Rights and Responsibilities*, 94th Cong., 2nd sess., p. 207.

2. Robert S. Stevens and Harry G. Henn, *Cases and Materials on the Law of Corporations* (St. Paul: West Publishing Co., 1965), pp. 307–312.

3. Hugh L. Sowards, *Corporation Law: Cases and Materials* (New York: Matthew Bender Co., 1974), sec. 1.02.

4. C. T. Carr, ed., *Select Charters of Trading Companies* (London: The Selden Society, 1913), pp. xiv–xv.

5. Ralph Nader, Mark Green, and Joel Seligman, *Constitutionalizing the Corporation: The Case for the Federal Chartering of Giant Corporations* (Washington, D.C.: Corporate Accountability Research Group, 1976), p. 424; R. Nader, "The Case for Federal Chartering," p. 81.

6. Harry Aubrey Toulmin, Jr., *A Treatise on the Anti-Trust Laws of the*

United States (Cincinnati: W. H. Anderson Co., 1949), 1:26–32.

7. Stuart Bruchey, "Corporation: Historical Development," in *The Changing Economic Order: Readings in American Business and Economic History*, ed. Alfred D. Chandler, Stuart Bruchey, and Louis Galambos (New York: Harcourt, Brace & World, 1968), pp. 140–144; see also James Willard Hurst, *The Legitimacy of the Business Corporation in the Law of the United States, 1780–1970* (Charlottesville, Va.: University Press of Virginia, 1970), pp. 13–57.

8. Bruchey, op. cit., p. 143.

9. Adolf A. Berle, Jr. and Gardiner C. Means, *The Modern Corporation and Private Property*, rev. ed. (New York: Harcourt, Brace & World, 1968), pp. 120, 127.

10. Armand Budington DuBois, *The English Business Company After the Bubble Act, 1720–1800* (New York: Commonwealth Fund, 1938); Bishop Carleton Hunt, *The Development of the Business Corporation in England, 1800–1867* (Cambridge: Harvard University Press, 1936); L. C. B. Gower, "Some Contrasts Between British and American Corporation Law," *Harvard Law Review* 69 (1956):1369.

11. Shaw Livermore, *Early American Land Companies: Their Influence on Corporate Development* (New York: Commonwealth Fund, 1939); Joseph S. Davis, *Essays in the Earlier History of American Corporations* (Cambridge: Harvard University Press, 1917), 1:25–27.

12. Shaw Livermore, "Unlimited Liability in Early American Corporations," *Journal of Political Economy* 43 (1935):674 (italics added).

13. Frederick W. Maitland, "Introduction," in Otto von Gierke, *Political Theories of the Middle Ages* (Cambridge: Cambridge University Press, 1900), p. xxxviii.

14. Arthur W. Machen, Jr. *A Treatise on the Modern Law of Corporations* (Boston: Little, Brown & Co., 1908), 1:18.

15. Adolf A. Berle, Jr., *Cases and Materials on Corporation Finance* (St. Paul: West Publishing Co., 1930), p. 43.

16. Ibid. (italics added).

17. Adolf A. Berle, Jr. and William C. Warren, *Cases and Materials on the Law of Business Organizations* (New York: Foundation Press, 1948), p. 1.

Chapter 4

1. Alan R. Bromberg, *Crane and Bromberg on Partnership* (St. Paul: West Publishing Co., 1968), p. 4.

2. Frederick G. Kempin Jr., "The Corporate Officer and the Law of Agency," *Virginia Law Review* 44 (1958):1273.

3. Cf. Ayn Rand, *The Virtue of Selfishness: A New Concept of Egoism* (New

York: New American Library, 1963), chaps. 12–13.

4. Frederick W. Maitland, "Introduction," in Otto von Gierke, *Political Theories of the Middle Ages* (Cambridge: Cambridge University Press, 1900), p. xxiv.

5. Wesley Newcomb Hohfeld, "Nature of Stockholders' Individual Liability for Corporate Debts," *Columbia Law Review* 9 (1909):288 (italics in original).

Chapter 5

1. Ralph Nader, Mark Green, and Joel Seligman, *Taming the Giant Corporation* (New York: W. W. Norton Co., 1976), pp. 75–76.

2. Ibid., pp. 100–102.

3. Ralph Nader, Mark Green, and Joel Seligman, *Constitutionalizing the Corporation: The Case for the Federal Chartering of Giant Corporations* (Washington, D.C.: Corporate Accountability Research Group, 1976), pp. 199, 204.

4. Nader et al., *Taming the Giant Corporation*, pp. 121–128.

5. Ibid., p. 128.

6. Nader et al., *Constitutionalizing the Corporation*, p. 226; Nader et al., *Taming the Giant Corporation*, pp. 148–150, 173–175.

7. Nader et al., *Taming the Giant Corporation*, pp. 129–130.

8. Ralph Nader, Mark Green, and Joel Seligman, "The Myth of Corporate Democracy," *Washington Monthly*, July/Aug., 1976, p. 54.

9. Nader et al., *Taming the Giant Corporation*, p. 81.

10. Testimony of Ralph Nader, June 17, 1976, in U.S. Congress, Senate, Committee on Commerce, *Hearings: Corporate Rights and Responsibilities*, 94th Cong., 2nd sess., p. 203.

11. Nader et al., *Taming the Giant Corporation*, p. 75.

12. Ibid.

13. Harry G. Henn, *Agency, Partnership and Other Unincorporated Business Enterprises* (St. Paul: West Publishing Co., 1972), pp. 38–40.

14. For an historical example of a president being censured by the board for exceeding his authority, see my book *Steel Titan: The Life of Charles M. Schwab* (New York: Oxford University Press, 1975), p. 128.

15. Nader et al., *Taming the Giant Corporation*, p. 37.

16. Edmund S. Morgan, "The American Revolution: Who Were 'The People'?", *New York Review of Books*, Aug. 5, 1976, pp. 32–33.

17. See chap. 3 and the sources cited in chap. 3, n. 7.

18. J. C. Ayer, *Some of the Usages and Abuses in the Management of our Manufacturing Corporations* (Lowell, Mass., 1863), p. 3 (italics added). A

copy of this rare work can be found in the library of the Graduate School of Business, Stanford University.

19. Gray v. President, Directors & Company of Portland Bank, 3 Mass. 363 (1807). For other early nineteenth-century cases in which the courts explicitly applied partnership principles to corporations, see E. Merrick Dodd, *American Business Corporations Until 1860* (Cambridge: Harvard University Press, 1954), p. 18, n. 6; p. 25, n. 35; pp. 66, 69. For a recent criticism of the preemptive-rights doctrine, see Z. Cavitch, *Business Organizations* (New York: Matthew Bender, 1971), vol. 6, sec. 115.01(2), esp. nn. 22 and 23.

Chapter 6

1. "Playboy Interview: Ralph Nader," *Playboy*, Oct., 1968, p. 76.

2. Peter H. Schuck, "The Nader Chronicles," *Texas Law Review* 50 (1972):1465–1466.

3. Daniel St. Albin Greene, "An Unflattering Look at Nader—and His Response," *National Observer*, Aug. 28, 1976, p. 10.

4. *Harvard Law Record*, March 26, 1976, p. 3.

5. *Wharton Magazine*, Fall 1977, p. 64.

6. Patrick Young, "A Legion of Press Agents," *National Observer*, Aug. 28, 1976, p. 10.

7. Nader, Letter-to-the-Editor, *National Observer*, Sept. 18, 1976, p. 12, italics added.

8. Robert Hessen, "Creatures of the State? The Case Against Federal Chartering of Corporations," *Barron's*, May 24, 1976, p. 7.

9. Ralph Nader, Mark Green, and Joel Seligman, *Constitutionalizing the Corporation: The Case for the Federal Chartering of Giant Corporations* (Washington, D.C.: Corporate Accountability Research Group, 1976), pp. 77, 447.

10. Nader's citation reads: Federal Trade Commission, *Report on Utility Corporations*, No. 69A, at 76, Sept. 15, 1934. The correct citation is: Federal Trade Commission, *Compilation of Proposals and Views For and Against Federal Incorporation or Licensing of Corporations*, S. Doc. No. 92, 70th Cong., 1st Sess., pt. 69-A, at 76 (1934).

11. Nader, June 16, 1976, responding to a question at a Georgetown Law Center conference on federal chartering; Mark Green, Letter-to-the-Editor, *Barron's*, Aug. 2, 1976, p. 7.

12. Irving Brant, *James Madison: The Nationalist, 1780–1787* (Indianapolis: Bobbs-Merrill Co., 1948), 2:363–369; Irving Brant, *James Madison: Father of the Constitution, 1787–1800* (Indianapolis: Bobbs-Merrill Co., 1950), 3:149–150; James Madison, *Journal of the Federal Convention*, ed.

E. H. Scott (Chicago: Albert, Scott & Co., 1893), pp. 725−726; Max Ferrand, ed., *Records of the Federal Convention* (New Haven: Yale University Press, 1937), 2:321−325, 615−616.

13. Ralph Nader, Mark Green, and Joel Seligman, *Taming the Giant Corporation* (New York: W. W. Norton Co., 1976), p. 66; Ralph Nader, "The Case for Federal Chartering," in *Corporate Power in America*, ed. Nader and Green (New York: Grossman Publishers, 1973), p. 74.

14. Nader et al., *Taming the Giant Corporation*, p. 37.

15. Ibid.

16. Adolf A. Berle, Jr. and Gardiner C. Means, *The Modern Corporation and Private Property*, rev. ed. (New York: Harcourt, Brace & World, 1968), p. 126.

17. Ibid., p. 127.

18. Nader et al., *Taming the Giant Corporation*, p. 43−44.

19. Lincoln Steffens, "New Jersey: A Traitor State," *McClure's* 25 (May 1905):41−45. For Abbett's dates in office, see Roy R. Glashan, comp. *American Governors and Gubernatorial Elections, 1775−1975* (Stillwater, Minn.: Croixside Press, 1975), p. 210.

20. Steffens, loc. cit.

21. Henry R. Seager and Charles A. Gulick, Jr., *Trust and Corporation Problems* (New York: Harper & Bros., 1929), p. 361−362; Archibald H. Stockder, *Business Ownership Organization* (New York: Henry Holt & Co., 1922), p. 203; James Bonbright and Gardiner C. Means, *The Holding Company* (New York: McGraw-Hill Book Co., 1932), p. 57.

22. Robert E. Cushman, "James B. Dill," in *Dictionary of American Biography* (New York: Charles Scribners Sons, 1930), 5:309; New Jersey Laws of 1889, chap. 265.

23. Nader et al., *Taming the Giant Corporation*, p. 44.

24. Steffens, op. cit., p. 44.

25. Nader et al., *Taming the Giant Corporation*, pp. 44−45.

26. Harold W. Stoke, "Economic Influences Upon the Corporation Laws of New Jersey," *Journal of Political Economy* 30 (1930):551.

27. Richard N. Owens, *Business Organization and Combination* (New York: Prentice-Hall, 1934), p. 502, reports that New Jersey did not enact its first antitrust statute until 1913; Seager and Gulick, op. cit., pp. 342−343, presents a list of every state which passed an antitrust law prior to the enactment of the Sherman Act of July, 1890; their list does not include New Jersey.

28. Nader et al., *Taming the Giant Corporation*, p. 269, unnumbered footnote.

29. Edward Q. Keasbey, "New Jersey and the Great Corporations,"

Harvard Law Review 13 (1899):198, 209.

30. Ibid., pp. 209–212.

31. Nader et al., *Taming the Giant Corporation*, pp. 50–52.

32. Ibid., p. 52.

33. Stockder, op. cit., pp. 162–163; the same point was made again in Russell C. Larcom, *The Delaware Corporation* (Baltimore: Johns Hopkins Press, 1937), pp. 29–30. Cf. New Jersey Laws, 1898, chap. 172, and 21 Delaware Laws, 1899, chap. 273, sec. 8.

34. Berle and Means, op. cit., p. 127.

35. Nader et al., *Taming the Giant Corporation*, p. 239.

36. Nader, *"The Case for Federal Chartering,"* p. 85.

Chapter 7

1. Henry G. Manne, "Mergers and the Market for Corporate Control," *Journal of Political Economy* 73 (1965):110.

2. Burton G. Malkiel, *The Debt-Equity Combination of the Firm and the Cost of Capital* (New York: General Learning Press, 1972), p. 4.

3. Ralph Nader, Mark Green, and Joel Seligman, *Constitutionalizing the Corporation: The Case for the Federal Chartering of Giant Corporations* (Washington, D.C.: Corporate Accountability Research Group, 1976), p. 169.

4. Ibid., p. 356 (italics added); Ralph Nader, Mark Green, and Joel Seligman, *Taming the Giant Corporation* (New York: W. W. Norton & Co., 1976), p. 216.

5. Compare Nader et al., *Taming the Giant Corporation*, p. 53 with pp. 29–30 and with *Constitutionalizing the Corporation*, p. 356.

6. Nader et al., *Taming the Giant Corporation*, p. 90.

7. Ibid., pp. 158–159.

8. Keith V. Smith, "The Increasing Stream Hypothesis of Corporate Dividend Policy," *California Management Review* 14 (1971):56–57.

9. Nader et al., *Constitutionalizing the Corporation*, p. 295; *Taming the Giant Corporation*, pp. 136–139, 173–179.

10. Nader et al., *Constitutionalizing the Corporation*, p. 295.

11. Nader et al., *Taming the Giant Corporation*, p. 138; *Constitutionalizing the Corporation*, pp. 293–295.

12. *New York Times*, Jan. 24, 1971, sec. 3, p. 9.

13. Nader et al., *Constitutionalizing the Corporation*, p. 289.

14. Nader et al., *Taming the Giant Corporation*, p. 138.

15. Hale v. Henkel, 201 U.S. 43, 74.

16. Ibid., p. 75.

Chapter 8

1. Ralph Nader, Mark Green, and Joel Seligman, *Taming the Giant Corporation*, (New York: W. W. Norton & Co., 1976), p. 209.

2. Ibid., pp. 213–214; Ralph Nader, Mark Green, and Joel Seligman, *Constitutionalizing the Corporation: The Case for the Federal Chartering of Giant Corporations* (Washington, D.C.: Corporate Accountability Research Group, 1976), p. 353.

3. Nader et al., *Taming the Giant Corporation*, p. 27.

4. Ibid., pp. 151, 208.

5. Ibid., pp. 215–216.

6. Ibid., p. 32.

7. Ibid., p. 38.

8. George Rogers Taylor, *The Transportation Revolution, 1815–1860* (New York: Holt, Rinehart & Winston, 1951), pp. 132–140, 153–175; Fred M. Jones, *Middlemen in the Domestic Trade of the United States, 1800–1860* (Urbana: University of Illinois Press, 1937), pp. 44–58.

9. Nader et al., *Constitutionalizing the Corporation*, pp. 34–35; the last word is changed to "increased" in Nader et al., *Taming the Giant Corporation*, p. 38–39.

10. Taylor, op. cit., pp. 209–210; Victor S. Clark, *History of Manufactures in the United States* (New York: McGraw-Hill, 1929), 2:496–500; Fritz Redlich, *History of American Business Leaders: Iron and Steel* (Ann Arbor: Edwards Bros., 1940), pp. 35–47, 91–102.

11. See Thomas L. Berg, *Mismarketing: Case Histories of Marketing Misfires* (Garden City, N.Y.: Doubleday & Co., 1970).

12. Thomas R. Navin, "The 500 Largest American Industrials in 1917," *Business History Review* 44 (1970):360.

13. Nader et al., *Constitutionalizing the Corporation*, pp. 506–531.

14. Nader et al., *Taming the Giant Corporation*, p. 220.

15. Ibid., p. 151.

16. Ibid., p. 152.

17. Ibid., p. 153.

18. The most glowing comment about Alcoa's ability was made by the judge who ruled that it was an illegal monopoly. (See Judge Learned Hand's opinion, United States v. Aluminum Co. of America, 148 F. 2nd 416 [1945].)

19. Nader et al., *Taming the Giant Corporation*, p. 233.

20. Ibid., pp. 234–235; Nader et al., *Constitutionalizing the Corporation*, pp. 386–388.

21. Nader et al., *Constitutionalizing the Corporation*, p. 385 (italics added); Nader et al., *Taming the Giant Corporation*, p. 233, changes "any

line of commerce" to "any important line of commerce."

22. Nader et al., *Taming the Giant Corporation*, p. 256.

23. Ibid., p. 210.

24. U.S. v. E.I. DuPont de Nemours & Co., 351 U.S. 377 (1956).

25. See D. T. Armentano, *The Myths of Antitrust* (New Rochelle, N.Y.: Arlington House, 1972).

Chapter 9

1. Ralph Nader, "The Case for Federal Chartering," in *Corporate Power in America,* ed. Ralph Nader and Mark J. Green (New York: Grossman Publishers, 1973), pp. 79, 83, 85.

2. Ralph Nader, Mark Green, and Joel Seligman, *Taming the Giant Corporation* (New York: W. W. Norton & Co., 1976), pp. 239, 240–241, 255.

3. Nader, "The Case for Federal Chartering," p. 85.

4. Nader et al., *Taming the Giant Corporation*, p. 255.

5. Ibid.

6. Interview with Mark Green, "Federal Chartering of Corporations: The Idea You Love to Hate," *MBA*, July/Aug., 1976, p. 24.

7. Nader, "The Case for Federal Chartering," p. 83.

8. Nader et al., *Taming the Giant Corporation*, p. 240.

9. Ibid., p. 241.

10. Christopher Scanlan, "New Controls on the Corporate Giants?", *Juris Doctor,* Nov. 1976, p. 52.

11. Ibid., p. 55.

12. Nader, "The Case for Federal Chartering," p. 79 (italics added).

13. Ralph Nader and Mark J. Green, "Is the 'Worldcorp' Above the Law?", *War/Peace Report*, Sept./Oct., 1973, pp. 6–7.

14. Ibid., p. 7.

15. Nader et al., *Taming the Giant Corporation*, p. 240.

16. Ibid., p. 241; Ralph Nader, Mark Green, and Joel Seligman, *Constitutionalizing the Corporation: The Case for the Federal Chartering of Giant Corporations* (Washington, D.C.: Corporate Accountability Research Group, 1976), p. 394.

17. Nader et al., *Taming the Giant Corporation*, pp. 240–241.

18. Nader et al., *Constitutionalizing the Corporation*, p. 391.

19. Nader et al., *Taming the Giant Corporation*, p. 240.

20. Ibid.

21. Chester M. Rohrlich, *Organizing Corporate and Other Business Enterprises* (New York: Matthew Bender Co., 1967), p. 75; Alan R. Bromberg,

Crane and Bromberg on Partnership (St. Paul: West Publishing Co., 1968), pp. 168–170.

22. *Fortune,* May 1976, pp. 223–224.

23. Nader et al., *Constitutionalizing the Corporation,* pp. 506–531.

24. Nader et al., *Taming the Giant Corporation,* p. 254.

25. Ibid., pp. 17, 181, 235.

26. Ibid., p. 17.

27. Ayn Rand, *Capitalism: The Unknown Ideal* (New York: Signet, 1967), pp. 46–48.

28. David Ignatius, "The Stages of Nader," *New York Times Magazine,* Jan. 18, 1976, p. 54.

29. "Interview: Ralph Nader," *Rolling Stone,* Sept. 20, 1975, p. 57.

30. Alexander Cockburn and James Ridgeway, "Ralph Nader Forecasts Big Change Coming in the 1980's," *Village Voice,* Sept. 29, 1975, p. 19.

31. Charles McCarry, *Citizen Nader* (New York: Saturday Review Press, 1972), p. 313; *New York Times,* Jan. 24, 1971, sec. 3, p. 9.

32. *Village Voice,* Sept. 29, 1975, p. 19.

33. *New York Times,* Jan. 24, 1971, sec. 3, p. 9.

34. Peter H. Schuck, "The Nader Chronicles," *Texas Law Review* 50 (1972):1464.

35. J. L. Talmon, *The Origins of Totalitarian Democracy* (New York: Frederick A. Praeger, 1961), p. 42.

36. The 1971 essay was first published as "Socialism as a Pluralist Commonwealth," in *The Capitalist System: A Radical Analysis of American Society,* ed. Richard C. Edwards (Englewood Cliffs, N.J.: Prentice-Hall, 1972), pp. 524–537; it was reprinted, with addenda, as "Notes toward a Pluralist Commonwealth," in Staughton Lynd and Gar Alperovitz, *Strategy and Program: Two Essays Toward a New American Socialism* (Boston: Beacon Press, 1973), pp. 49–109.

37. Gar Alperovitz and Jeff Faux, "After the Corporation," *New York Times,* June 28, 1976, Op. Ed. page; "Nader 'Disappointed' by Carter's Choices," *San Francisco Chronicle,* Dec. 8, 1976, p. 15; Sandra Hochman, "America's Chronic Critic Ralph Nader Finally Has the President's Number," *People,* Feb. 28, 1977, p. 84; Jeremy Rifkin and Ted Howard, "Alperovitzian Economics," *New Times,* March 18, 1977, pp. 18–19.

38. Alperovitz, "Notes Toward a Pluralist Economy," p. 59.

39. Ibid., pp. 59–62.

40. Ibid., p. 87.

41. Ibid., p. 85.

42. Ibid., p. 88.

Index

Abbett, Leon, 68–70
Adhesion, contract of, 55
Advertising, 89, 91–94, 109
Agency powers, 37–39, 53–56
Aggregate, partnership as, 15, 41
Alperovitz, Gar, 113–14
American Revolution, 28
Annual meetings, 45, 56
Antimonopoly court, 95
Antitrust laws, 96–97
Articles of incorporation, 3, 25–26, 38–40
Artificial legal entity, corporation as, xiv, 15, 22, 41

Bankruptcy, 94
Barriers to entry, 94
Berle, Adolf A., Jr., xii, xv, 16–17, 18, 31–32, 43, 64, 67, 72
Blackstone, Sir William, 5, 9
Boroughs, medieval, 5–6
Bromberg, Alan R., 17, 39
Bruchey, Stuart, 28
Bubble Act (1720), 29–30
Business trusts, 80, 106, 107

Capital, 42–43, 79–80
Capitalism, xii–xiii, xvii
Catholic Church, 107–8
Certificate of incorporation, 4, 26
Charitable trusts, medieval, 8–9
Charter, corporate, 25–33 passim
Churches, medieval, 7–8
Close corporations, 20–21
Coke, Sir Edward, 9

Collective guilt of giant corporations, xvii, 85, 103
Commenda, 44
Common Law, 9–10
Competing products, 92–93, 94, 96
Competition, 89–97 passim
Competitive challenges, 91–93
Community-owned enterprises, 112–14
Concentration ratios, 94, 95–97
Concessions, 28
Concession theory of corporations, xiii–xiv, 4–8 passim, 9–11, 31–33
Connecticut, Act of 1837, 29, 67, 72
Contractual theory of corporations, 16–18, 29–30, 31–32, 43–46, 55
Constitutional safeguards, xiv–xv, 84–85
Constitutionality of federal chartering, 64–65
Constitutionalizing the Corporation (Nader, Green & Seligman), xvi, 63–64
Constructive notice, 39–40
Cooperatives, 106, 107
Corporate democracy, 50–53, 56–59, 108
Corporate features created by contract, 16–18, 29–30, 31–32, 43–46, 55
Corporate features without incorporation, 17, 29–30, 107
Corporation: defined by Blackstone, 5–6; by Coke, 9; by Marshall, 9, 22

Corporation, medieval concept of,
    4–11 passim
Corporations de facto, 29–30
Creditors, expectations and entitle-
    ments, 37–40 passim

Dahl, Robert, xiii
Dartmouth College case (1819), 9
Defining an industry, difficulty of,
    95–97, 102
Delaware corporation law, 71–75
Delectus personae, 38
Delegation of agency powers, 39,
    53–56
Dill, James B., 68–70
Direct notification to creditors,
    39–40
Directors, 39, 50–51
Discretionary authority of corporate
    president, 53–56
Disney, Walt, 79
Dispersion of share ownership, 45,
    82
Dissolution of giant corporations,
    95–97, 112
Diversification of investments, 80–81
Divestiture decrees, 95
Dividends, 81–83
Division of labor, 43, 79
DuPont cellophane case, 96–97

Economic power, compared to
    political power, 109–11
Enforced equality, 113–14
Entity status, 15, 16–17
Entity theory, 15, 20–21, 22, 41–42
Extortion in feudal system, 4, 10

Federal chartering of corporations,
    xvi–xvii, 50–52, 64–65, 74–75,
    101–2, 105–9
Federal chartering as weapon against
    media, 108–9
Federal chartering agency, proposed,
    101
Fictitious legal person, corporation
    as, xiv, 15, 22
Fifth Amendment, 85
Financial intermediaries, 82–83,
    92–93

First Amendment, 108
Foreign corporations, subject to
    federal chartering, 105
Fourth Amendment, 85
Fourteenth Amendment, xiv, 85
Free transferability of shares, 30, 42

Galbraith, John Kenneth, xii
General incorporation statutes, 3,
    25–26, 29, 66–68, 72–73
General partners, 44
Geographical monopolies, 90–91
Godkin, E. L., 111
Goebel, Julius W., Jr., 10
Going public, 55, 79
Golden age of competition, 90–91;
    of corporate democracy, 57
Gouge, William, 29
Green, Mark, xvi, 64, 102
Guilds, medieval, 6–7

Hand, Learned, 89
Hohfeld, Wesley Newcomb, xiv, 46
Holding companies, 69–70

Idle capacity, 90
Individual rights, 40–42, 45–46,
    115
Information, availability and use by
    shareholders, 49, 51–52
Inherence theory of corporations,
    xiv, 18, 22. See also Contractual
    theory of corporations
Institutional investors, 82–83
International chartering of corpora-
    tions, 104–5
Investors, corporate, 42–45, 79–81
Iron Law of Wages, 115

Jacksonian critics of chartered
    monopolies, 29, 66
Joint stock companies, 10, 29

Keasbey, Edward Q., 70–71, 72
King, consent to incorporate, 3
Kristol, Irving, xi–xii
Kyd, Stewart, 9

Land, Edwin, 79
Legal barriers to entry, 94

Leggett, William, 29
Legislative approval for incorporation, 3
Legislative role under general incorporation statutes, 33
Legitimacy of corporations, xi–xii, xvii
Limited liability, 16, 17–18, 39, 41, 107; for torts, 18–21, 41
Limited partners, 44, 80
Limited partnership, 44, 107
Liquidity for investors, 42, 81
Livermore, Shaw, xiv, 30

Machen, Arthur W., Jr., 31
Madison, James, 65–66
Maitland, Frederick W., xiv, 31, 42
Malkiel, Burton G., 81
Management, specialized skills contributed by, 80
Managing partner, 43
Manne, Henry G., 81
Market shares, 95–97, 102
Marburgh, Theodore F., 90
Marriage, procedural requirements for, 26
Marshall, John, 9, 22
Means, Gardiner C., xii, xv, 67, 72
Media, as targets of federal chartering, 108–9
Medieval concept of corporations, 4–11 passim
Modern Corporation and Private Property (Berle and Means), xii, 67, 72–73
Monopoly, 89–97 passim
Morawetz, Victor, xiv
Morgan, Edmund S., 56
Mueller, Willard F., xiii
Mutual agency powers, of partners, 37–38; absence in corporation, 39

Nader, Ralph: as critic of corporations, xv–xvi; proposes federal chartering as remedy, xvi; proposed changes, xvii; on corporations as recipients of special privileges, 15; concept of corporate charter, 25; theory of rights, 27; concept of "the public interest," 25, 32; criticism of state incorporation laws, 49–50; on corporate autocracy, 49; shareholders deprived of information, 49; on selection of directors, 50–51; on compulsory disclosure of information, 51, 83–84; advocates shareholder plebiscites, 52; on corporate democracy as ideal, 52; on corporate democracy as legal norm, 53; on passive role of shareholders, 56; reputation for accuracy, 63–64, 73; on James Madison as advocate of federal chartering, 65–66; on general incorporation statutes, 66–67; on New Jersey's corporation laws, 68–71; on Delaware's corporation laws, 71–73; advocates dual chartering, 74; on dividends withheld from shareholders, 81; on dispersion and concentration of shareholding, 82; on monopolistic behavior of giant corporations, 89; on stagnation of giant corporations, 89; on competition in pre-Civil War era, 90–91; on advertising and thrift, 92; on corroboration of advertising claims, 93, 109; favors dismantling of giant corporations, 95; proposes Antimonopoly Court, 95; proposes new test of monopoly power, 95; discrepancies in 1973 and 1976 proposals for federal chartering, 101–2; criteria for federal chartering coverage, 102–3; proposes international chartering, 104–5; includes foreign corporations under federal chartering, 105; includes privately held corporations under federal chartering, 106; exemptions from federal chartering, 106–7; on giant corporations as "private governments," 109; political philosophy, image of model citizen and ideal society, 111–13
National railroad network, impact on competition, 90–91
New Jersey corporation law, 68–71, 73

Non-profit corporations, 106—8

Officers, agency powers of, 39
One-man corporations, 20—21

Parliament, consent to incorporate, 3
Partnership: dissolution, 15; un-
    limited liability, 16, 19, 21;
    durability, 17; entity status, 17;
    features, 37—38, 57—58; historic
    origins, 38
Perpetual duration of corporations,
    15, 17
Plebiscites, 52, 81
Political metaphors applied to corpo-
    rations, 52, 109—10
Political power compared to econom-
    ic power, 109—11
Poole, A. L., 4
Precedents, Common Law theory of,
    9—10
Predictability under state incorpora-
    tion laws, 74—75
Preemptive rights, 57—58
President, authority of corporate,
    53—56
Prescriptive role of state incorpora-
    tion laws, 55
Presumption of innocence, 85, 103
Privacy, corporate right to, 83—85
Private governments, corporations
    as, 109—10
Private property, corporations as,
    xii—xiii
Privately held giant corporations,
    106
Procedural requirements for incor-
    poration, 26
Pyramidal image of corporation, 53

Quasi-governmental agencies, corpo-
    rations as, 28, 29, 66

Raiders, corporate, 81
Railroads, impact on competition, 91
Rand, Ayn, 110
Ratification of agency authority, 54
REIT (real estate investment trusts),
    107

Relevant product markets, 95, 102
Respondeat superior, 19
Restrictions on transferability of
    partnership interests, 38, 42
Retained earnings, 81, 83
Retroactive authority, 54
Rights of corporations, xiv—xv, 40—
    42, 45—46, 115
Rousseau, Jean Jacques, 113

Savings, as alternative to spending,
    92—93
Secrecy. See Privacy
Sedgwick, Theodore, 29
Seligman, Joel, xvi, 103
Separation of ownership and control,
    xii, 42—43, 79—80, 107
Shareholders, 42—43, 45, 49—53,
    58—59, 79—81
Sherman Act (1890), 97
Size of corporations, 58, 97, 102—3,
    106, 115
Size, relationship between legal form
    and, 107
Smith, Adam, xi—xiii
Smith, Keith V., 83
Social Contract (Rousseau), 113
Socialist criticism of capitalism, 115
Soviet citizens, compared with status
    of shareholders, 52
Specialization of function, 42—43, 79
Stagnation by giant corporations, 89,
    92, 94
State-prescribed formalities for
    incorporation, 38—40
State role under general incorpora-
    tion statutes, 3, 25—26, 39—40,
    49—50, 53, 66—67, 73—75
Steffens, Lincoln, 68—69
Stock exchange, 58—59
Stoke, Harold W., 69—70
Suppletory role of state incorpora-
    tion laws, 55
Sutton's Hospital case (1613), 9

Takeover attempts, 81
Talmon, J. L., 113
Taming the Giant Corporation (Nader,
    Green and Seligman), xvi, 63—65

Tax-farmers, 5
Tort liability: of partners, 19; of
    shareholders, 19
Torts, 18–21
Trade secrets, 84
Trusts. See Charitable Trusts and
    Business Trusts

Unemployment, 90
United Nations, Group of Eminent
    Persons, 104

Vethake, John, 29

Vicarious liability, 19–20
Void for vagueness, 97
Voluntary association, corporation
    as, 40, 45
Voter participation, 18th century,
    56–57

Watson, Thomas, J., 79
Wilgus, H. L., 64
Williston, Samuel, 7
Wilson, Woodrow, 73

About the Author

Robert Hessen is a historian educated at Queens College, Harvard University and Columbia University. He taught in the Graduate School of Business at Columbia University until 1974. Since then he has been a research fellow at the Hoover Institution and teaching in the Graduate School of Business, Stanford University. He is the author of *Steel Titan: The Life of Charles M. Schwab* (Oxford University Press, 1975).